Keeping Hearth and Home in Old COLORADO

A Practical Primer for Daily Living

compiled and edited by
Carol Padgett, Ph.D.

MENASHA RIDGE PRESS
BIRMINGHAM ✦ ALABAMA

Copyright © 2002 by Carol Padgett
All rights reserved
Manufactured in the United States of America
Published by Menasha Ridge Press
Distributed by The Globe Pequot Press
First edition; first printing

Library of Congress Cataloging-in-Publication Data
is available from the Library of Congress

Cover design by Grant M. Tatum and Bud Zehmer
Text design by Grant M. Tatum and Annie Long

Menasha Ridge Press
P.O. Box 43673
Birmingham, AL 35243
(205) 322-0439
www.menasharidge.com

ISBN: 0-89732-524-9

Contents

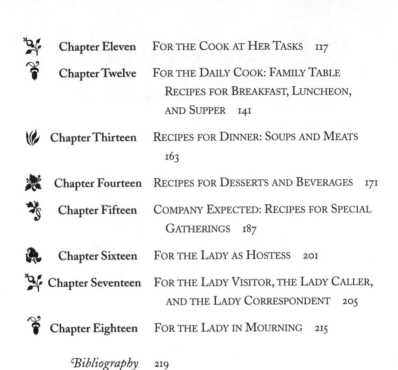

Acknowledgments

I have shaped *Keeping Hearth & Home* at a keyboard rather than a pastry board, with ingredients pulled from library shelves rather than kitchen shelves. Yet, the process of preparing this nineteenth-century buffet of recipes and "receipts," mores and maxims has been reminiscent of growing up in my grandmother's kitchen.

Any attempt to assign proper measure to those who have assisted in the preparation of this nineteenth-century buffet seems as fruitless as my grandmother's efforts to leave us the legacy of her cornpones. Trying valiantly to render a recipe, she tossed each ingredient into a bowl and noted its quantity with care. Alas, there is no measure for a cook's intuition or the size of her palm. And there is no way to aptly express my gratitude for the many who enriched this effort.

Menasha Ridge Press Publisher Bob Sehlinger entrusted me with this bill of fare. Ann Nathews, library director for Southern Progress Corporation, like a generous neighbor offering a "starter batch," enriched my garden of ingredients, and Birmingham Public Library staffer Shirley Nichols delivered a steady stream of nineteenth-century delectables. Development Editor Carolyn Carroll, bless her heart, culled my gleanings and arranged the buffet table with impeccable taste, and Associate Publisher Molly Merkle and Managing Editor Gabriela Oates made sure dinner "got in the oven" on time. Tricia Parks ingeniously brought our harvest to market.

My husband Ben encouraged me by donning an apron and purchasing a hand-held scanner. From the other end of our Marital Computer Table, he added the secret ingredients of perspective and humor. New friends and old have opened doors of Colorado history with the hospitality of old mountaineers. Karen Delaney Gifford, assistant archivist at University of Colorado at Boulder and a fourth-generation Coloradoan, mined Denver's libraries and Leadville's pantries as well as her own family papers. Between stints at the copier, she even noted recipes whose ingredients were seasonal staples in Colorado's high altitudes. Other generous assistance was offered by Steve Fisher at the University of Denver, Jessy Randall at Colorado College, Jim Chipman at the Colorado State Archives, and Jean Settles at the Colorado Historical Society.

Lillian Echols Eggers cheered from afar and pointed me to local resources. Susan Crow, executive director of Denver Urban Ministries, stirred interest that yielded suggestions whose variety rivaled the dishes at a congregational potluck dinner. Lorraine Kirkland single-handedly served a feast of leads. Colorado Public Radio producer Laura Carlson offered to solicit information from listeners; and Dan Drayer conducted a delightful interview on the "Colorado Matters" program of which he is executive producer and host.

Colorado women of the nineteenth century have been my companions and mentors. Their handwritten recipes and published advice have provided glimpses into the principles with which they nourished their relationships and the practices by which they ordered their lives. Their quaint language and homespun truths have stirred my heart; and our hearthside conversations have seasoned my soul. As one of our nineteenth-century forebears said upon presenting a similar book, "I have enjoyed the task heartily, and from first to last the persuasion has never left me that I was engaged in a good cause."

—Carol Padgett

Introduction

Keeping Hearth & Home in Old Colorado is a lovingly constructed anthology of homemaking advice culled from a wealth of mid- to late nineteenth-century cookbooks, household manuals, and periodicals. It is, in essence, a greatest-hits album of the domestic wisdom of the time, a simpler time, a time without (for most Coloradoans) electricity, telephones, automobiles, supermarkets, and countless other conveniences we take for granted today. My passion for capturing the wisdom of this age resides in my lifelong fascination with the everyday lives of those who came before me: What was it like to live then? What were the tasks and pleasures that filled the hours of each day? I have always treasured the old-time literature of the home as a tender personal keepsake, much like the legacy of handwritten recipes and hand-stitched finery that my female predecessors left behind.

It is my hope that *Keeping Hearth & Home* will bring the lives of your great- or great-great-grandmothers to light, for this is how they lived; and this book is one they might have consulted when in need of just the right recipe for calf tongue or for a trustworthy treatment for a colicky infant, had such a comprehensive collection as this been available during their day. Instead, our forbears depended on a variety of such sources to help them manage the multiple roles of their demanding home lives. They thumbed through receipts in the addenda of period cookbooks for tips on tending to the upkeep of their home, the needs of the sick, and the dietary requirements of the young. They studied etiquette books to master the finer points of proper deportment and social propriety. They awaited the arrival of hometown "weeklies" and national "monthlies"—such as *Godey's Lady's Book*, *Harper's Bazaar*, and *Scientific American*—for advice on maintaining a moral atmosphere in the home. This book brings representative tidbits from all these sources together.

Domestic advice literature connected women to the broader society and assisted them in examining and shaping their individual lives. In fact, the genre became so pervasive that *The Enterprising Housekeeper*, written in 1897, noted that it was "almost the fashion to apologize for taxing a much-abused public with the burden of a new book on this subject." Yet how grateful I am for the abundance of this literature that enlightens us about the lives of our ancestors. In addition to educating and charming me, our nineteenth-century sisters have humbled me with wisdom for which our twentieth and twenty-first centuries have often claimed credit. It seems, more accurately, that women through the ages have agreed on a number of basic principles for orchestrating a home, harmonizing a marriage, and fine-tuning the children. As you shake your head at the quaintness of one practice—A married gentleman shows respect for his wife by speaking of her as "Mrs." and never as "my wife"—or feel your skin prickle at the ignorance of outmoded mores—A lady is at her best when she exhibits a modest and retiring manner—you will also, surprisingly, often marvel at the modern-day wisdom of other instructions—Better to live in one room, with all the furniture your own, than occupy a whole house with scarcely a chair or a table paid for.

As its title implies, the book offers its advice in the context of home and hearth, for that is the context in which most nineteenth-century Colorado women lived. In the second half of the nineteenth century, Colorado's earlier domination by unmarried male prospectors gave way to families drawn from all parts of the world, and Colorado's reputation assumed an air of gentility. When Colorado joined the Union in 1876 as the "Centennial State," historian Frank Fossett described the state's population, "now of a settled and permanent character," as one "unsurpassed for intelligence, enterprise, thrift, and energy," with educational and religious facilities of the highest order and schools and churches unequalled in their liberality. The state, whose population and wealth had tripled since the advent of the railways in 1870, entered the Union as The Switzerland of America, The World's Sanitarium, and Sportsman's Paradise. Fossett hailed Colorado as a state where "in the midst of the finest scenery the world can produce, the invalid obtains a new lease of life, the tourist finds a world of attractions, and the sportsman a harvest no other land can furnish."

"There is an abundance here," said Ernest Ingersoll of Colorado. Colorado's breathtaking landscape touched the heart of Katherine Lee Bates, a New England school teacher, who wrote "America the Beautiful" while standing atop Pike's Peak in 1893. Platte Canyon inspired Walt Whitman during the same decade to pen the poem "Spirit that Formed This Scene." Abundance filled pockets as well as hearts. Early miners had translated Colorado's state motto "Nil Sine Numine," which means "Nothing without Providence," as "Nothing without a New Mine." Although the Gold Rush brought the first rush of settlers to Colorado, silver was often "the immense wealth delved from the crevices of her rocky frame." The Chicago World's Fair in 1893 featured the world's largest piece of silver, discovered east of Aspen. Colorado silver filled Butch Cassidy's pockets when he robbed the Telluride Bank in 1889 and escaped with $30,000. Culinary abundance filled pockets as well. In 1871, O. P. Batter invented the ice-cream soda in Denver. In the 1890s, Henry Perky developed a process of pressing wheat into strips, which he baked into restaurant biscuits and sold door-to-door as Shredded Wheat.

Keeping Hearth & Home in Old Colorado attempts to convey the delight of discovering and living amidst such abundance while also juggling the multiple demands of the home and ranch. Here are featured not only the advice women would have received but also period recipes—as preserved in the congregational and community cookbooks that proliferated in the state between the end of the Civil War and the turn of the century—and numerous accounts of daily life by women in various circumstances.

With the advent of ready-made clothing and laborsaving machinery, women's lives began to extend to areas previously exclusive to men. Over 800 women supervised ranches as "cattle queens" during the 1880s, and others successfully managed farms. Colorado also lays claim to three notorious women gamblers: Poker Alice Tubbs,

Calamity Jane Bourke, and Killarny Kate, all reputed to smoke mammoth stogy cigars while playing cards. In 1893, Colorado followed Wyoming—but preceded all other states—in granting women the right to vote. A female poet celebrated the suffrage vote in The Western Clubwoman: "It was sentimental nonsense, thus in poetry impearled; for the hand that casts the ballot is the hand that rules the world." Colorado women celebrated their voting privileges in the next general election by placing three of their number in the General Assembly.

 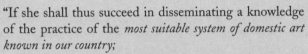

"If she shall thus succeed in disseminating a knowledge of the practice of the *most suitable system of domestic art known in our country;*

if she shall succeed in lightening the labors of the housewife by placing in her reach a guide which will be found *always trusty and reliable;*

if she shall thus make her tasks lighter and home-life sweeter;

if she shall succeed in contributing something to the health of American children by instructing their mothers in the art of preparing light and wholesome and palatable food;

if she, above all, shall succeed in making American homes more attractive to American husbands, and spare them a resort to hotels and saloons for those simple luxuries which their wives know not how to provide;

if she shall thus add to the comfort, to the health and happy contentment of these, she will have proved in some measure a public benefactor, and will feel amply repaid for all the labor her work has cost."

—Marion Cabell Tyree, 1877

CHAPTER ONE

———◆———

$\mathcal{F}$OR THE LADY WELL GROOMED AND WELL DRESSED

Guidelines for Grooming

BE TIDY. Young girls, don't allow yourselves to fall into untidy habits. There is nothing more displeasing than an untidy woman, old or young: hair full of dust, shoe buttons pinned on, nails with black rims, clothes ill-fitting—basted and pinned. In fact, there is no limit to the untidiness that a person will fall into who is given to this sort of thing.

STOCK YOUR TOILET. No matter how humble your room may be, there are eight things it should contain: mirror, washstand, soap, towel, comb, hair-, nail-, and tooth-brushes. These are just as essential as your breakfast, before which you should make good use of them.

SET A WEEKLY BATH. A set time for each member of the family to take a weekly bath will promote the convenience of the household. Saturday night and Sunday morning are the best times for most persons. The weekly bath thus becomes a preparation for Sunday-morning toilet, which is ordinarily the most careful and elaborate of the week.

USE COLD WATER. If begun in summer, as we suggest, there is no danger of contracting a cold from the bath, and as the weather gradually grows colder in the fall, no shock will come to the already acclimated system. Then, even though the sleeping room should be so cold that ice forms in the pitcher during the night, the morning bath will be taken without a shudder, and the healthy glow that follows will be more than a reward for the resolution, time, and effort it costs.

BATHE WITH RAIN WATER. Rain water is the best by far to use for the toilet. Little or no soap is needed with it, as it is very soft and easily removes all dirt.

☞ *Pamper Your Body* ☜

- ❈ Think deliberately of the house you live in—your body.
- ❈ Make up your mind firmly not to abuse it.
- ❈ Eat nothing that will hurt it; wear nothing that distorts or pains it.
- ❈ Do not overload it with victuals, drink, or work.
- ❈ Give yourself regular and abundant sleep.
- ❈ Keep your body warmly clad.
- ❈ At the first sign of danger from the thousand enemies of health that surround you, defend yourself.
- ❈ Do not take cold; guard yourself against it. If you feel the first symptoms, give yourself heroic treatment.
- ❈ Get into a fine glow of heat by exercise. Take a vigorous walk or run, then guard against a sudden attack of perspiration.
- ❈ This is the only body you will ever have in this world. A large share of the pleasure and pain of life will come through the use you make of it.

⚙ Study deeply and diligently the structure of your body, the laws that should govern it, and the pains and penalties that will surely follow a violation of every law of life or health.

—*The Household Guide or Domestic Cyclopedia*, 1902

WASH WITHOUT SHAMPOO. The head should be washed at least once a week, but shampooing is a great detriment to the beauty of the hair. Soap fades the hair, often turning it yellow. Brushing is the only safe method of removing dust from the head, with the occasional use of the whites of eggs when washing.

CLEAN THE TEETH DAILY. Cleanliness will preserve and beautify any teeth, unless they are actually diseased. All pastes and toothwashes should be discarded. Do not use the highly advertised preparations, however delightful they are. Chalk and myrrh are excellent and safe dentifrices, as is Castile soap.

ALWAYS WEAR GLOVES WHEN:

- 🌼 **HOUSEKEEPING.** If a lady desires a soft, white hand, she should always wear gloves when performing her household tasks.

- 🌼 **OUTDOORS.** A lady must guard against the elements.

- 🌼 **SLEEPING.** Sleeping in soft, white kid gloves after rubbing mutton tallow on the hands will keep hands soft and white, as large mittens filled with wet bran or oatmeal will ward off the disfiguring effects of housework.

Eat well. Ladies who wish clear complexions, instead of using cosmetics, eat vegetables and fruit, as long as they are in season; and never throw away cucumber water or the juice of any fruit, but rub your face with it whenever you have it.

☛ *Suitable Exercises for Females* ☚

Running. To strengthen abdominal muscles, run, lifting your feet high, like a spirited horse.

Skipping. There is some prejudice against this form of exercise from the fact that it can be overdone, and also from the popular idea that it is injurious to girls to jump. If they are properly dressed, and their muscles are gradually developed, and they use good common sense as to their amount of exercise, there are practically no dangers in skipping.

—What a Young Woman Ought to Know, 1898

Miscellaneous Recipes—Skin and Face

To make fine cologne water. Into a bottle, drop the following oils: 1 dram each of lavender and bergamot, 2 drams each of lemon and rosemary, 8 drams each of cinnamon and cloves, and 50 drams of tincture of musk. Cork and shake well.

To cure moist hands. Some people have moist, clammy hands that are very disagreeable to the touch. Exercise, plain living, and the local application of starch powder and lemon juice will cure this affliction.

☛

One-half pint of bay rum, 3 tablespoonsful of glycerine, 3 of white Castile soap, shaved and then dissolved in ½ pint of soft water. After washing and drying the hands, rub on a little until dry.

—Our Kitchen Friend, 1889

TO WHITEN ARMS. For an evening party or theatricals, rub arms with glycerine, and before the skin has absorbed it all, dust on refined chalk.

TO FORTIFY AGAINST WRINKLES. The hand of time cannot be stayed, but his marks upon the face need not be placed there prematurely. One of the best local treatments consists in bathing the skin frequently in cold water and then rubbing with a towel until the flesh is aglow. A little bran added to the water is a decided improvement. This treatment stimulates the functions of the skin and gives it vigor. Wrinkling may be further remedied by washing the parts three times a day with a mix of 4 drams glycerine, 2 drams tannin, 2 drams rectified spirits, and 8 ounces water.

TO REMOVE FRECKLES. Many ladies are very much annoyed at freckles, but we have seen faces on which they were positive beautifiers.

[9]

Probably the best eradicator of these little blemishes, known as *Unction de Maintenon*, is composed of Venice soap dissolved in lemon juice, with oil of bitter almonds, deliquidated oil of tartar, and, after it has turned to ointment in the sun, oil of rhodium. Bathe the freckled face at night with this lotion, and wash the face in the morning with clear, cold water, or if convenient, with a wash of elder flower and rose water. A little lemon juice and milk mixed together and applied nightly will also remove freckles.

Miscellaneous Recipes—Hair

TO WARD OFF GRAY HAIR. We can only counsel moderation in those pleasures that tend to an exciting, unhealthy mode of living, but here is a recipe that a writer believes will prevent graying: Melt 4 ounces pure hog's lard (unsalted) and 4 drams spermaceti, and when cool, add 4 drams oxide of bismuth. Perfume to suit.

HAIR-CURLING LIQUID FOR LADIES. Take 2 ounces borax and 1 dram gum Senegal in powder; add 1 quart hot water. Stir and add 2 ounces spirits of wine strongly impregnated with camphor. On retiring to rest, wet the locks with the liquid and roll them on twists of paper as usual. Leave them till morning, when they may be unwrapped and formed into ringlets.

☞ *Remedy for Dandruff* ☜

There is no simpler or better remedy for this vexatious appearance (caused by a dryness of the skin) than a wash of camphor and borax. An ounce of each put into a pint and a half of cold water, and afterwards rub a little pure oil into the scalp.

—*Our Kitchen Friend*, 1889

To CLEANSE THE HAIR. Break the whites of two eggs into a basin of soft water and work them up to a froth in the roots of the hair. Rinse thoroughly with clean warm water.

When the hair can be worn perfectly plain and still be becoming, one is counted specially fortunate, but as very few faces can stand this a very short fringe is still worn, which, while it is not tightly curled, is made fluffy. The single curl in the centre of the forehead, so much fancied by French women, has not the vogue of last season. Every one wants to be able to part the hair, wear a little jeweled comb at each side and twist it softly either high or low on the neck, for this is not only the most fashionable, but the most artistic style, and is valued accordingly.

—"The Small Belongings of Dress," in *The Ladies' Home Journal*, April 1894

Miscellaneous Recipes—Teeth

To CARE FOR THE TEETH. Salt and water cure tender gums. In the early stages, vinegar will remove tartar, but if it remains too long it has a tendency to loosen the teeth. Never use a pin or any metal substance to remove food that lodges between the teeth. Food and drinks that are too hot or too cold will destroy the beauty of the teeth.

To CLEAN THE TEETH. Rub them with the ashes of burnt bread. The juice of the strawberry is a natural dentifrice.

To FASTEN THE TEETH. Put powdered alum, the quantity of a nutmeg, in a quart of spring water for 24 hours, then strain the water and gargle with it.

TO CURE FOUL BREATH. A gargle made of a spoonful of chloride of lime dissolved in a half tumbler of water will sweeten the breath. Bad breath also can be rendered less disagreeable by rinsing the mouth with Horsford's Acid Phosphate.

To Clean the Teeth

A leaf of pure simple sage is the best tooth brush and preserver that nature or science has given to man. Keep a sage plant in the house, if you have not a garden from which to pluck it at all times. The sage leaf may be used fresh or dry. A drop or two of myrrh may be added to the water with which the mouth is rinsed after the sage leaf friction, as it strengthens the gums and imparts a pleasant odor to the breath. When sage cannot be obtained, white curd soap is excellent for cleansing the teeth.

—*Good Housekeeping in High Altitudes*, 1888

Both ladies and gentlemen will be very careful to keep their breaths sweet and pure. We wish there were a law to prevent people from polluting their breaths with onions and tobacco when going into mixed company. No one has a right to make himself in any manner offensive to others. All the laws of good breeding forbid it. The taint of smoking can be overcome by chewing common parsley. The odor imparted by garlic and onions may be much diminished by chewing roasted coffee grains, parsley leaves, or seeds.

—Anna R. White, *Youth's Educator for Home and Society,* 1896

Guidelines for Dressing

DRESS FOR THE AFTERNOON. Make it a rule of your daily life to improve your toilet after dinner work is over and to "dress up" for the afternoon. A girl with fine sensibilities cannot help feeling embarrassed and awkward in a ragged and dirty dress and with her hair unkempt should a neighbor come in. Moreover, your self-respect should demand the decent appareling of your body. You should make it a point to look as well as you can, even if you know nobody will see you but yourself.

KEEP YOUR UNDERCLOTHING IN PERFECT ORDER. Wear shields, such as the Union Undergarments now so much in use, under the sleeves of every dress; if you perspire much between the shoulders, place a square of light flannel next to the skin to absorb perspiration and keep the body from the danger of sudden drafts.

MEND CAREFULLY. If you have but three calico frocks, you can be as neat as if your wardrobe boasted of silk and satin gowns. Examine every garment when it comes from the wash, and, if necessary, mend it with neatness and precision. Do not sew up the holes in your stockings, as we have seen some careless, untidy girls do, but take in a broad margin around the hole, be it small or large, with a fine darning needle and darning cotton. Cover the fracture with an interlaced stitch so close as to be strong as the body of the stocking and fine enough to be ornamental. Never let pins do duty as buttons or strings take the place of proper bands.

Dress for Mountaineering

… a half-fitting jacket, a skirt reaching to the ankles, and full Turkish trousers gathered into frills which fall over the boots—thoroughly serviceable and feminine costume for mountaineering and other rough traveling in any part of the world.

—Isabella L. Bird, *A Lady's Life in the Rocky Mountains*, 1881

By seven o'clock Mrs. Gray was in her corner, dressed in black silk, with purple ribbons in her cap, and some fine knitting in her hand. Catherine, a brunette, wore a pink silk fastened with black-velvet rosettes, and with puffed sleeves of black Spanish lace. Clara's dress was white cambric striped with pale green. She wore in her hair sprigs of the pale smilax; an old-fashioned gold chain, with a square, red-jeweled ornament, clasped her slender throat and long ear-rings.

—"The Tea-Party," in *Appletons' Journal,* October 1871

ALWAYS DRESS SIMPLY. A true lady does not adopt gay and showy colors and load herself down with jewelry which is entirely out of place and conveys a very great anxiety to "show off." Your dress may, or need not, be anything better than calico, but with a ribbon or flower or some bit of ornament, you can have an air of self-respect and satisfaction that invariably comes with being well dressed.

SELECT SIMPLE ACCESSORIES. Never carry coarse embroidered or laced handkerchiefs. Fine, plain ones are much more ladylike. Avoid open-worked stockings and fancy slippers. For special occasions, fine, plain, white hose and black kid slippers, with only a strap of rosette in front, are more becoming. Otherwise, wear thick-soled

It is in very bad taste, indeed, to wear bracelets outside of your gloves on the street. Although very many fashionable women wear their bracelets outside of their gloves in the evening, the propriety of it has always been questioned. Three or four strands of small gold beads make the prettiest necklace for a young girl, unless she should be fortunate enough to possess pearls, which, of course, are specially suited to youth and innocence.

—"The Small Belongings of Dress," in
The Ladies' Home Journal, April 1894

shoes, and in damp or raw weather always protect your limbs; either wear leggings or an extra pair of stocking legs.

SCENT YOUR ACCESSORIES NOT YOURSELF. The scented French glove boxes are sufficient in themselves, sometimes, but if a liquid be used, let it be as sparingly as possible. I only seek to impress upon my lady friends the truth of the old proverb as applied to perfumes: "Too much of a good thing is good for nothing." A handkerchief saturated with coarse eau de cologne or a strong essential oil marks a person as possessing very little good taste.

SUIT YOUR BONNET TO YOUR FACE. If one has a long slender face, the bonnet should be arranged to make a soft framing; if one has a broad, full face, the bonnet should be sufficiently large, and its trimmings arranged to give a high rather than a wide effect. Ties should always be worn, even if because of a plump throat they have to be very narrow. Nothing gives a woman quite so ridiculous an air as an unsuitable bonnet.

AVOID THE TIGHT BODICE, IF STOUT. The average dressmaker who attempts to make a gown for a stout woman makes it as close fitting as possible—as bare of trimming as can be. Nine times out of ten, even if she makes the sleeves full at the top, she fits them in, after the manner of a glove, below the elbow, so that every particle of flesh on the arm is held down, and the hands are extremely red. The result of a tight-fitting bodice is a red face, consequently the stout woman should not wear one, but instead should select that which, while it fits her well, also permits every ounce of flesh to stay in its proper place.

AVOID THE TIGHT SKIRT, IF STOUT. Equally unbecoming to the stout woman is a tight-fitting skirt, and for that reason one with not only a little fullness around the top but also with a fold or two arranged across the front is advised. The stout woman should remember that trimmings carried up to the shoulder, high sleeves, and bretelle effects all have a tendency to increase the height, and that should be her aim in dressing.

Beware the Corset

... the corset or tight clothing can do most damage to the vital organs below the diaphragm. The largest of these is the liver. ... When Hiram Powers, the great sculptor, was in this country, he once attended an elegant party, and was observed watching very intently a beautifully dressed, fashionable woman. A friend, noticing his interest, said to him, "What an elegant figure she has, hasn't she?" "Well," said Powers, "I was wondering where she put her liver."

—*What a Young Woman Ought to Know*, 1898

SPORT QUIET COLORS. New or bizarre colors are considered the privilege of the very young woman. Flaring blues, brilliant greens, glowing pinks, or deep yellows seldom look well on a middle-aged woman. She can always wear rich, deep colors; and that she is being catered to nowadays is shown by the popularity of royal purple, of deep petunia, and of the daintiest grays imaginable. Black and white are always in good taste.

BALIN & RANSOHOFF

Miscellaneous Recipes—Caring for Clothing

TO TEND STAINS. The principal stains and spots the laundress has to reckon with are tea, coffee, wine, iron rust, ink, paint, tar, grass, mildew, blood, grease, and mud stains. These should all be removed from washable articles before sending them to the laundry. Hence many housekeepers set apart Tuesday for wash day, and take occasion Monday to sort the wash and carefully remove all stains, and sponge, scrub, or dry clean any articles that may require it.

TO CLEAN LACE. Stretch the lace carefully on a thick piece of wrapping paper, fastening the edges with pins. Sprinkle it thickly with calcinated magnesia, cover with another piece of wrapping paper, and place it under a pile of books or other heavy weight for three or four days. The magnesia can then be shaken off, and the lace will appear like new.

November 15, 1871... Went over to Mrs. C's and did a quantity of washing; it was hard work; and I am to iron the things tomorrow. When I first arrived I found that washing, done very badly, would not at all suit my ideas. So my kind neighbour, Mrs. C., offered me the weekly use of her wash-tubs and irons; and after scorching a few collars, getting into a state of black despair with the starch, rubbing the skin off my knuckles with the rubber, and burning my hands with the irons, I have turned into quite a good laundress. Many are the pleasant mornings we spend over our wash-tubs, while she tells me stories of her life in beautiful California and Oregon. ...

*—South by West or Winter in the Rocky Mountains
and Spring in Mexico, 1874*

TO KEEP MOTHS FROM CLOTHING. Put a few cuttings of Russia leather in your trunk or wardrobe or sprinkle a few peppercorns, pimento corns, or cloves in the same places.

To Clean Kid Gloves

Have ready a little new milk in one saucer, and a piece of brown soap in another, and a clean cloth or towel, folded three or four times. On the cloth spread out the glove smooth and neat. Take a piece of flannel, dip it in the milk, then rub off a good quantity of soap on the wetted flannel, and commence to rub the glove toward the fingers holding it firmly with the left hand. Continue this process until the glove, if white, looks of a dingy yellow, though clean; if colored, till it looks dark and spoiled. Lay it to dry, and the operator will soon be gratified to see that the old glove looks nearly new. It will be soft, glossy, smooth and elastic.

—Darley Family Papers, 186?

January, Wednesday 8, 1890
Oh such work, and such a lot of dirty clothes. I got them ready for the line, the wind so hard, yet I managed to hang all out. The tub frozen full of water, I worked at 2 hours before I could get enough of it out so I could put the clothes in.

January, Friday 17, 1890
I got my clothes on the line. It broke and they all went into the dirt. I never lost my temper but took them up, put them into the tub, finished as best I could . . .

March, Saturday 15, 1890
I hung the few things I could on the fence, the wind blew all down. I had them to do over.

—Emily French, *Emily—The Diary of a Hard-Worked Woman*

Recommendation for Washing Clothes

If I were to be asked by one who was a new beginner what in my judgment was the best way to secure peace, long life, and happiness in the family, I would first ask, "Have you a clothes wringer?" If not, I would then be ready to give my advice. Taking care to let conscience rule, I would say, "Get as one of the first and most essential things Way's Patent Lever Clothes Wringer," and then give my reasons, which are many:

1. It is the most durable and simple in its construction.

2. Its superiority of rolls.

3. No thumb screws, cogs, or springs to rust and get out of order.

4. Its rolls adjust themselves to any thickness of cloth, from a bed quilt to thinnest lace, merely by the pressure of the foot.

5. Your tub cannot tip over, as it is not fastened to the wringer but on one of the best commodities that can grace a laundry, a bench neat and handy, so that a child can readily work it.

In fact, time nor space would allow the naming of all there is to be said in praise of this, the woman's friend. It has taken the premium and two prize medals at the Cincinnati Exposition, 1873–74 and first premium at the State Fairs of Ohio. In fact it gives splendid satisfaction. Everybody likes it. It is the common sense wringer.

—Advertisement in *Centennial Buckeye Cook Book,* 1876

Chapter Two

---

*F*or the Lady Well Comported

Cultivate Personal Carriage and Grace

Carry yourself with grace. The beauties of the charming picture framed by a lady's dress are enhanced by her graceful movement. To walk with style is rare enough, but when it comes to sitting down in a dress properly—well, there are not many social graces equal to that.

Keep your arms from going astray. A question often comes up, not so easily answered: What shall I do with my hands and arms? Some ladies always carry a fan. But you cannot always have one in your hands, so it is better to keep the arms pressed lightly against the sides in walking or sitting. This position for the hands, although a little stiff at first, will soon become easy and graceful. Ladies should never adopt the ungraceful habit of folding their arms or of placing them akimbo.

Cultivate your manners. A lady should:

☢ Be quiet in her manners, natural and unassuming in her language, careful to wound no one's feelings, but giving generously and freely from the treasures of her pure mind to her friends.

🧠 Scorn no one openly but have a gentle pity for the unfortunate, the inferior, and the ignorant, at the same time carrying herself with an innocence and single-heartedness which disarms ill nature and wins respect and love from all.

🧠 Such a lady is a model for her sex, the "bright particular star" on which men look with reverence. The influence of such a woman is a power for good which cannot be overestimated.

FIND YOUR MUSICAL VOICE. The sound of a discreet and well-modulated voice is a power in itself. Cultivate a low, clear tone of voice and an easy conversing manner free of gesticulation. Regular features cannot be cultivated, but a kindly expression can be cultivated and so, too, can a pleasant voice.

☞

Slang phrases seem to be *à la mode* in this 19th century; and they issue from rosy lips which appear almost incapable of such guile. We will not repeat the fashionable slang, thereby, perhaps, spreading its serpent trail more widely, but merely allude to the too frequent repetition of "See here," "Hold on," and "I say," wherewith not only callow school girls, but even young ladies who are of so-called aristocratic tendencies and "out in society," delight to adorn their peculiar phraseology.

—A Manual of Etiquette with Hints on Politeness and Good Breeding, 1873

Mind Your Demeanor in Social Exchanges

LIMIT YOUR OBSERVATIONS. A quiet person is seldom disliked, while a noisy one sets the nerves all in motion and at war with each other and causes one to feel, in parlance popular, "like flying." Noise, the disturber, deranges the mental faculties and incapacitates the mind for clear and deliberate thought. A boisterous, loud-talking man is disagreeable enough, but a woman who falls into the habit is almost unendurable. Many times have we seen an inoffensive husband tucked completely out of sight by the superabundant flow of volubility proceeding from his wife, who, we like to believe, is by nature intended to be the gentler and restraining element.

RESIST SLANG. The use of slang is becoming unbearable. Girls are unable to express themselves in standard language, and slang is growing more and more vulgar. It used to have the merit of a little wit, even if a poor kind, but now it is often a meaningless jingle; and worse, it often carries a double meaning unknown to the speaker, which draws a smile, often of disgust, to the face of every man present.

Don't fall in love with her, Chase

As to what she is, you have seen for yourself—exceedingly pretty and free from the slightest approach to affectation, but awful "bad form" even for the West. Shoots, smokes, whistles, plays piano, writes poetry, and talks slang, gossips, does a good deed here and there, but, as she herself would phrase it, "out-bucks" every woman in Ranchtown, and is the leading character of the town. Now, don't fall in love with her, Chase; for I think of marrying her myself some day, when she reforms—as she undoubtedly will.

—Ella Rodman Church, "His Western Katharine,"
in *Appletons' Journal,* 1877

BE NOT EXCESSIVELY FRANK. Do not take pride in offensively expressing yourself on every occasion under the impression that you will be admired for your frankness. Speaking one's mind is an extravagance which has ruined many a person.

DO NOT BOAST. In company, do not converse with another in a language that is not understood by the rest. If you chance to use a foreign phrase, don't translate it. It is equivalent to saying, "You don't know anything." Never correct the pronunciation of a person publicly, nor any inaccuracy that may be made in a statement. Boasting of wealth, family, or position is exceedingly silly and tiresome to the listeners.

ALWAYS ACCEPT APOLOGIES. Only ungenerous minds will not do so. If one is due from you, make it unhesitatingly.

LISTEN. When a "tale of woe" is poured into your ears, even though you cannot sympathize, do not wound by appearing indifferent. True politeness decrees that you shall listen patiently and respond kindly.

LAUGH AT APPROPRIATE TIMES. Don't laugh, when a funny thing is being said, until the climax is reached. Do not laugh at your own wit; allow others to do that.

USE TACT WHEN ADMONISHMENT IS NECESSARY. Tact is needed in a friend to show us our weaknesses; also with employers and parents. Many do harm instead of good in their manner of rebuking, wounding instead of rousing the self-respect of those they reprimand!

RESIST THE URGE TO GOSSIP. A gossip is more or less malicious and uncultivated; if nothing worse, she is empty-headed. Do not hold up the peculiarities of absent friends to ridicule or discuss them uncharitably. Never speak disparagingly of another or rejoice in another's misfortune; it will be charged to envy. News that is not well vouched-for should not be repeated; else you may acquire the reputation of being unreliable.

REFRAIN FROM EYEING OVER OTHER WOMEN. Few observant persons can fail to notice the manner in which one woman, who is not perfectly well bred or perfectly kind-hearted, will eye over another woman whom she thinks is not in such good society, and above all, not at the time being in so costly a dress as she herself is in. Who cannot recall hundreds of instances of that sweep of the eye which takes in a glance the whole woman and what she has on from top-knot to shoe-tie. It is done in an instant. No other evidence than this eyeing is needed that a woman, whatever be her birth or breeding, has a small and vulgar soul.

TREAT ENEMIES KINDLY. If you have an enemy and an opportunity occurs to benefit the person in matters great or small, do good service without hesitation. If you would know what it is to feel noble and strong within yourself, do this secretly and keep it secret. A person who can act thus will soon feel at ease anywhere. If enemies meet at a friend's house, lay aside all appearance of animosity while there and meet on courteous terms.

KISS SPARINGLY. Many times a contagious disease has been conveyed in a kiss. The kiss is the seal of pure and earnest love and should never be exchanged save between nearest and dearest friends and relatives. Indeed, public sentiment and good taste decree that even among lovers it should not be so often indulged in as to cause any regret on the part of the lady should an engagement chance to be broken off. Let promiscuous kissing, then, be consigned to the tomb of oblivion

On the Street

❧ Ladies in our country are allowed considerable freedom in receiving and paying visits and can appear in the daytime in all public places unattended by their brothers, husbands, or friends of either sex. They can also attend public exhibitions, libraries, etc., and appear on the promenades alone, but this is not the case either in Paris or London.

❦ Walk in an easy, unassuming manner, neither looking to the right or to the left, nor walking too quickly. If anything in a store window attracts a lady's notice, she can stop and examine it with propriety and then resume her walk.

❦ In bowing on the street, a lady must merely incline her head gracefully and not her body. But she should always smile pleasantly. It lights up the features and adds a refreshing warmth to the greeting.

❦ Do not chew gum on the streets.

❦ In passing people on the walk, turn to the right.

❦ Do not join forces with three or four others and take up the entire pathway, compelling everyone to turn out for you. Walk in couples when there are several friends in your party.

❦ Do not pass between two persons who are talking together.

❦ Do not introduce people in a public conveyance. It draws attention to a person and makes him unpleasantly conspicuous.

❦ Do not seize hold of a piece of goods which another customer is examining, but wait until she has either made her purchase or passed it by.

❦ Do not pass in or out of the general entrance of a hotel but by the ladies' entrance only.

Chapter Three

---

*F*or the Young Lady Courted and Escorted

While Escorted

LADIES, CARRY SOME ARTICLES. The parasol, when that is necessary as a sun shade, must not be borne by the gentleman unless because of sickness or old age the lady requires peculiar assistance. A lady at a ball should not burden a gentleman with her gloves, fan, and bouquet to hold while she dances, unless he is her husband or brother.

ALLOW THE ESCORT TO ATTEND ALL WHILE TRAVELING. When traveling with an escort, a lady should not concern herself with any of the details of her trip. It is presumed that her escort knows more about traveling than she does, and it will annoy him to be continually asked about the safety of baggage, whether they are on the right train, and numberless other fussy questions that would scarcely be excusable in children. The lady or her relatives should supply the escort with sufficient money to defray all her expenses. Some prefer to have the gentleman attend to these matters and settle the account at the end of the journey, but a strict record of all the items should be kept in this case.

A Lady's Life in the Rocky Mountains

His face was remarkable. He is a man about 45, and must have been strikingly handsome. He has large grey-blue eyes, deeply set, with well-marked eyebrows, a handsome aquiline nose, and a very handsome mouth. His face was smooth-shaven except for a dense moustache and imperial. Tawny hair, in thin uncared-for curls, fell from under his hunter's cap and over his collar. One eye was entirely gone, and the loss made one side of the face repulsive, while the other might have been modeled in marble. ... I almost repented of having sought his acquaintance. His first impulse was to swear at the dog, but on seeing a lady he contented himself with kicking him, and coming up to me he raised his cap, showing as he did so a magnificently-formed brow and head, and in a cultured tone of voice asked if there were anything he could do for me. I asked for some water, and he brought some in a battered tin, gracefully apologising for not having anything more presentable. We entered into conversation, and as he spoke I forgot both his reputation and appearance, for his manner was that of a chivalrous gentleman, his accent refined, and his language easy and elegant. I inquired about some beavers' paws which were drying, and in a moment; they hung on the horn of my saddle. Apropos of the wild animals of the region, he told me that the loss of his eye was owing to a recent encounter with a grizzly bear, which, after giving him a death hug, tearing him all over, breaking his arm and scratching out his eye, had left him for dead. As we rode away, for the sun was sinking, he said, courteously, "I hope you will allow me the pleasure of calling on you."

—Isabella L. Bird, *A Lady's Life in the Rocky Mountains,* 1881

Dancing

At private dances a lady must not decline the invitation of a gentleman to dance, unless she is previously engaged or does not intend to dance any more during the evening. To do otherwise would be a tacit reflection upon the master and mistress of the house.

At a public ball, however, the master of ceremonies or the floor managers regulate the dancing, and they make many introductions, but should always remember to request the lady's permission to do so before introducing any gentleman to her.

Introductions at such places, one must remember, can, if desired, cease with the occasion. A lady is free to pass her partner of the previous evening, the next morning, without the slightest recognition, and he has no right to feel injured or annoyed.

—A Manual of Etiquette with Hints on Politeness and Good Breeding, 1873

Do not initiate long-term acquaintances on a trip. Feel free to make yourself agreeable to fellow passengers, if the journey will be long, without being misconstrued, but an acquaintance begun on a railway train should end there.

Go upon his arm to the hostess. If a gentleman accompanies a lady to a party or dance, he should always wait at the head of the stairs for her to come from the dressing room, and, descending the stairs first, he will be ready to offer his arm in the hall to escort the lady to the mistress of the house.

Learn the art of the horseback mount. The lady should place her left foot in one of her escort's hands, with her left hand upon his shoulder and her right hand on the pommel of the saddle. Then at a given word, she springs up, the gentleman at the same time raising his hand so that he assists her into the saddle. In riding, he should always keep on her right side.

LEARN THE ART OF THE BICYCLE MOUNT. The gentleman accompanying the lady holds her wheel; she stands at the left, places her right foot across the frame to the right pedal, which at the same time must be raised. Pushing this pedal causes the machine to start, and then with the left foot in place she starts ahead, very slowly in order to give her companion time to mount his wheel and join her. When their destination is reached, the gentleman dismounts first and appears at his companion's side to assist her; if she be a true American woman, she will assist herself as much as possible.

REST IF FATIGUED. During a walk in the country, ascending a hill, or walking on the bank of a stream, if the lady is fatigued and sits upon the ground, the gentleman does not seat himself by her but remains standing until she is rested sufficiently to proceed.

ACCEPT AID. A lady may accept the assistance of a strange gentleman in crossing a muddy or crowded street; such attentions should be accepted in the spirit in which they are offered and acknowledged with thanks.

While Courted

The essential requisites in a companion which are necessary to insure happiness and a life of devotion are to be found in strength of character, a healthy body, a judicious head, a loving heart, all brought into attune with a high and holy life purpose.

CULTIVATE YOUR TASTE FOR BOOKS. A taste for reading will always carry you to converse with men who will instruct you by their wisdom and charm you by their wit, who will soothe you when fretted and refresh you when weary, counsel you when perplexed and sympathize with you at all times.

IF YOU DESIRE HIM NOT, TELL HIM SO. If a lady perceives that she has become an object of special regard to a gentleman and does not incline to encourage his suit, she should not treat him rudely; but it is not well to let him linger awhile in suspense, and then bring him to the point only to be repulsed. Take an early opportunity to express your ideas upon the subject, in a way which will permit him to discover your sentiments.

BEHAVE SENSIBLY TOWARD HIM. And if you have accepted the addresses of a deserving man, do behave sensibly and honorably, and not lead him about as if in triumphal chains, nor take advantage of his love by playing with his feelings. Do not affect indifference to his presence and comfort, nor yet display too much affection for him while in the society of others.

The Two Lovers

Meanwhile, Katharine grew to womanhood, with all the beauty of a wild-rose, full of grace and gracelessness; and suitors far and near clamored for her hand. It was said that her father had never crossed her wishes, and that her temper was—well, whatever it was, it did not prevent Joe Carneth, the richest speculator in Colorado and owner of the Invincible, from laying fierce siege to the Ranchtown beauty. Joe was handsome, reckless, and generous; he loaded the girl with costly presents, he paid the old man's debts; and finally Katharine consented to marry him-though not without informing him, with her usual frankness, that she didn't love him, and didn't want to marry any one. This did not prevent her, however, from becoming Mrs. Carneth; but it probably saved her from any very serious grief when, two or three years afterward, her husband made such a melodramatic end, leaving her about as penniless as she was before.

—Ella Rodman Church, "His Western Katharine," in *Appletons' Journal,* 1877

LET LOVE AND REASON BE BLENDED. Reason is to love what a pair of spectacles is to a near-sighted man. Let your love be intelligent; mix your affection with brains. Reason enables the little fellow to look beyond the fair face and graceful form of his adored, beyond the festivities of the wedding and the beauties of the imagination, to the domestic fireside, to the kitchen comforts, to pudding, and the cash account. That's what reason conjoined with love will do!

BE EQUALLY YOKED. Marry your equal rather than your inferior or superior. Where there is great disparity—either socially, intellectually, financially, religiously, or in any other respect—disappointment and unhappiness are likely to be the result.

CHOOSE A MAN ONLY SOMEWHAT FAMILIAR WITH WOMEN. A woman should avoid accepting a man who has been particularly successful with women. At the same time, she should look for one to whom woman is not an enigma, and a man of the world and of strong character, so that she may feel sure that when he chose her, he said to himself: "I know my mind; happiness for me lies there."

STRAY FROM SPOILED MEN. A woman should avoid marrying a man who is the favorite of many sisters who constantly dance about in attendance on him. That man is spoiled for matrimony. He will require his wife to bestow on him all the attention he received from his sisters.

A French engaged couple are never allowed to be one instant alone together before marriage. ... I am so far from advocating this policy for American girls.

Let him pay his addresses to her undisturbed; let him say the sweet little foolish things which stir her heart so deeply, but which might stir your risibles; let him sing his love-songs to her and request her to meet him moonlight alone (alone, you observe!) with such expression as love gives the human voice, without your standing by in grim judgment on his performances, as if he were an opera-singer, and had charged you something for listening to him.

—*Get thee behind me, Satan!
A home-born book
of home-truths,* 1872

STRAY FROM THOSE TOO GOOD. I should advise you to shun a dragon of virtue like fire: a lady should prefer a dragoon rather. A man may be good, but he must not overdo it. He who has no wickedness is too good for this world; not even a nun could endure him. Fancy, my dear lady, a man being shocked by you! The male prig is the abomination of the earth, and should be the pet aversion of women.

To the Parents of the Courted Girl

CONSIDER SEXUAL COMPATIBILITY. Sometimes, even where a woman is endowed with fair physical powers and would make a helpful and congenial companion if she were equally mated, in her ignorance she consents to marry a man of great amative powers and of an insatiable sexual nature. The same result is inevitable when a man who is weak or of frail constitution and without powers of endurance marries a woman of strong physical powers and dominant sexual nature, whose sexual longings could not be satisfied except by a man who is equally strong and of like tendencies. Such unions oftentimes result in alienation and estrangement, and sometimes in unfaithfulness.

The Proposal

When the time for the proposal has come, your beloved might well consider these thoughts on how to proceed.

WHEN ASKING THE LADY. The mode in which the avowal of love should be made, must of course, depend upon circumstances. The heart and the head—the best and truest partners—suggest the most proper fashion. Station, power, talent, wealth, and complexion all have much to do with the matter; they must all be taken into consideration in a formal request for a lady's hand. If the communication be made by letter, the utmost care should be taken that the proposal be clearly, simply, and honestly stated. Every allusion to the lady should be made with marked respect. Let it, however, be taken as a rule that an interview is best, but let it be remembered that all rules have exceptions.

WHEN ASKING HER PARENTS. When a gentleman is accepted by the lady of his choice, the next thing in order is to go at once to her parents for their approval. In presenting his suit to them he should remember that it is not from the sentimental but the practical side that they will regard the affair. Therefore, after describing the state of his affections in as calm a manner as possible, and perhaps hinting that their daughter is not indifferent to him, let him at once, frankly and without waiting to be questioned, give an account of his pecuniary resources and his general prospects in life, in order that the parents may judge whether he can properly provide for a wife and possible family. A pertinent anecdote was recently going the rounds of the newspapers. A father asked a young man who had applied to him for his daughter's hand how much property he had. "None," he replied, but he was "chock full of days' work." The anecdote concluded by saying that he got the girl. And we believe all sensible fathers would sooner bestow their daughters upon industrious, energetic young men who are not afraid of days' work than upon idle loungers with a fortune at their command.

He did not speak for a moment. Then he drew nearer, looked with eager, questioning eyes into mine, and, reaching out his hand to me, said only, "Jenny, Jenny!" And then I put my hand in his, and for a moment he held it silently, yet firmly and tenderly, and, bending over, almost reverently, he touched it with his lips and said: "Darling, I will never hold it carelessly, and never, never let it go."

—"The Two Lovers," *in Appletons' Journal,* March 1871

BEHAVE ADMIRABLY WHILE ENGAGED. On your behavior toward your lover during your engagement will greatly depend the estimation in which you will be held by your husband in your married life. Many a wife has been made to feel the galling chains of matrimony by the husband, who, when a lover, was forced to acknowledge his fair fiancée's powers of torture. And on the other hand, the lover should not strive to annoy his lady love in order to discover whether she possesses a large share of good humor; but he should:

- Ever hold her as the queen of his heart, the only lady to whom his attentions are due.
- While in society make her pleasure and her amusement his first charge.
- Not keep close to her side as though held there by an invisible wire, yet manifest a desire to please her in all reasonable things.
- If he seeks the society of others, first see that she is with those who are friendly and agreeable to herself.

Ah! These Honeymoon Days Are Golden Days.

... The skies are radiantly beautiful. The carol of voluminous birds is merry music, and the beating heart keeps time to it. ... But when the honeymoon is over! What then? ... the skies darken and weep out their agony; the birds get sadly hoarse, as if with bronchitis, and the sad heart keeps tune to that.

... Can no fortunate compromise-ground be discovered between the domain of turtle-doves and snapping-turtles? ... Perhaps a courtship of generous length would be a sort of antidote to such immoderate "lovingness." ... A fortunate thing, also, would it be for the husband prospective, if, as a plighted lover, he were compelled ... to see his affianced petulant with pain, or nervously fretful with fever; to see her face woefully distorted with toothache; or, what is worse still, with her false teeth loosed from their moorings and entirely thrown aside. A lover who can stand these heroic tests will not be apt to fail in the day of calamity.

—"Ideal Womanhood," in *Overland Monthly and Out West Magazine*,
October 1871

CHAPTER FOUR

$\mathcal{F}$OR THE WIFE

Many a marriage has commenced like the morning, red, and perished like a mushroom. Wherefore? Because the married pair neglected to be as agreeable to each other after their union as they were before it.

TEND TO YOUR LOVE ABOVE ALL. If a man and a woman are to live together well, they must take the plant of love to the sunniest and securest place in their habitation. They must water it with tears of repentance, or tears of joy; they must jealously remove the destroying insects and pluck off the dead leaves, that the living may take their place. And if they think they have any business in this life more pressing than the care and culture of the plant, they are undeserving of one another, and time's revenges will be swift and stern. Their love vows will echo in their lives like perjuries; the sight of their love letters in a forgotten drawer will affect them with shame and scorn. In the bitterness of their own disappointment, they will charge God foolishly, thinking that every plant of love has a worm at the root because they neglected theirs and that every married life is wretched because they did not deserve happiness.

WIFE, LEAN UPON HIM. Be neither vexed nor ashamed to depend on your husband. Let him be your dearest friend, your only confidant.

WIFE, ATTEND TO HIM. In matrimony, to retain happiness and make it last to the end, it is not a question for a woman to remain beautiful, it is a question for her to remain interesting. Love feeds on illusions, lives on trifles. Not the slightest detail should be beneath her notice in order to keep alive her husband's attention. A rose on her head, her hair parted the other way, a newly trimmed bonnet may revive in him the interest he felt the first time he met her, nay, the emotion he felt the first time he held her in his arms.

Those blissful hours of courtship! Are they ever forgotten—the hand-pressure at the gate; the strolls under the elm-trees; the snatched kiss under the umbrella on that terrible rainy night? You know. Gracious! Don't I pity the married couple who can't look back on such sweet, fond, foolish pictures as this in memory's magic picture-book!

—*Get thee behind me, Satan!*
A home-born book
of home-truths, 1872

EXPECT WITHIN REASON. Hope not for constant harmony in the married state. The best husbands and wives are those who bear occasionally from each other sallies and ill humor with patient mildness. Be obliging, without putting great values on your favors. Hope not for a full return of tenderness.

RESPECT HIM. You need not be at pains to examine whether your husband's rights be well founded. It is enough if they are established. The affections of a husband are never to be gained by complaints, reproaches, or sullen behavior. Respect your husband's prejudices and his relations, especially his mother. She is not the less his mother because she is your mother-in-law; she loved him before you did.

Marriage and Toiletry

Now it may enchant a man once—perhaps even twice—or at long intervals—to watch his goddess screw her hair up into a tight and unbecoming knot and soap her ears. But it is inherently too unlovely a proceeding to retain indefinite enchantment. To see a beautiful woman floating in the deep, clear water of her bath—that may enchant for ever, for it is so lovely, but the unbeautiful trivialities essential to the daily toilet tend only to blur the picture and to dull the interest and attention that should be bestowed on the body of the loved one.

—Married Love, 1918

BE CHARITABLE, TOLERANT, AND HONEST:

- Never talk at one another, either alone, or in company.
- Never both manifest anger at once; if one is angry, let the other part the lips to give a kiss.
- Never speak loudly to one another, unless the house is on fire.
- Never find fault unless it is perfectly certain that a fault has been committed, and even then prelude it with a kiss, and lovingly.

- Never taunt with a past mistake or reflect on a past action which was done with a good motive and with the best judgment at the time.
- Never part without loving words to think of during absence; you may not meet again in life.
- Never deceive, for the heart once misled can never wholly trust again.

BE WORTHY OF TRUST AND DEFEND ONE ANOTHER. Once established in your home, preserve its affairs inviolate. You should have no friends save mutual ones, and those should never be made confidants of. Should anyone presume to offer you advice with regard to your husband or seek to lessen him by insinuations, shun that person as you would a serpent. Whether present or absent, alone or in company, speak up for one another, cordially, earnestly, lovingly. A man or woman who will speak slightingly of a life companion has outraged the first principles of happiness in the marriage relation—respect and politeness—and is not fit to be trusted.

☞ *Pet Him* ☜

Men, too, are at heart eternally children, and such tender petting as comforts children warms and sweetens a grown man's life. The "good night" should be a time of delightful forgetting of the outward scars of the years, and a warm, tender, perhaps playful exchange of confidences.

—Married Love, 1918

REGARD ONE ANOTHER SELFLESSLY. The very nearest approach to domestic felicity on earth is in the mutual cultivation of an absolute unselfishness. Let each one strive to yield oftenest to the wishes of the other. Neglect the whole world besides, rather than one another.

Never allow a request to be repeated; "I forgot" is never an acceptable excuse. Do not herald the sacrifices you make to each other's tastes, habits, or preferences. Let all your mutual accommodations be spontaneous, whole-souled, and free as air.

June, Wednesday 11, 1890

And I can scarcely contain the thought, am I really loved for the first time in my life—I so craved it now it is mine pure and true. I do try to not be foolish. I am in a new life. I am happy as I never expected to be.

Emily French, *Emily—The Diary of a Hard-Worked Woman*

In this respect I am inclined to think that man suffers more than woman. For man is still essentially the hunter, the one who experiences the desires and thrills of the chase, and dreams ever of coming unawares upon Diana in the woodlands.... I think that, in the interests of husbands, an important piece of advice to wives is: Be always escaping ... ensure that you allow your husband to come upon you only when there is delight in the meeting. Whenever the finances allow, the husband and wife should have separate bedrooms, failing that they should have a curtain which can at will be drawn so as to divide the room they share.

—Married Love, 1918

Matrimony and Finance

The husband should at the commencement of his married life tell his wife, as nearly as possible, the expected amount of his income; and together they should plan for its disbursement, in the most satisfactory manner to both.

A certain sum should be set aside for home expenses; rent, fuel, taxes, insurance, and all the minor details should be specified. The husband may take so much for his personal expenses and allow the wife a similar sum, also, setting aside a fund for contingent expenses.

When the items are all arranged with an eye to exactness (and accuracy is a cardinal virtue), the sum should be divided into monthly or weekly portions, and given regularly into the wife's hands; and the husband should not interfere with her department unless asked to do so.

If a man has married a decided simpleton or a spendthrift, he must make the best of his position, but if a woman of common discernment is thrown upon her own resources and given the purse, as well as the charge of household affairs, she rarely fails to develop good executive powers. The root of evil is in the failure on the part of the husbands to trust them, rather than on the part of the wives to execute their trust.

—A Manual of Etiquette with Hints on
Politeness and Good Breeding, 1873

CHAPTER FIVE

$\mathcal{F}$OR THE MOTHER, AS SHE COMFORTS AND CARES FOR THEM

Each wisely brought up and well-educated child is the best of all investments of a parent's wealth of money, affection, and effort.

Rules for Their Sleep

PROVIDE SEPARATE SLEEPING ENCLOSURES. Where should the infant sleep? Never in bed between the parents. When placed between the parents, the infant must constantly inhale the poisonous emanations from the bodies of two adults. It should sleep by the side of the mother's bed in a crib.

USE PROPER BEDDING. The best bed at all seasons of the year is one of oat straw. This is light and soft. It is better than hair, because the straw can often be changed and the tick washed. In cold weather, a thick woolen blanket should be doubled and spread over the straw bed to increase the warmth. For covering the little sleeper, woolen blankets should alone be used.

At Night

SILENCE and night were in the air,
I heard their whispers everywhere;
And wind-breaths through the wall-flowers went
Like unseen bees in search of scent.
Deep in the sky some stars were burning,
And then—I heard the round world turning!

—Enchanted Tulips and Other Verses for Children, 1914

USE PROPER PILLOWS. The pillow as well as the bed should be of straw. The heads of American children are for the most part little furnaces! I have seen scores of babies die of brain maladies, who would have recovered if their brains had not been baked in feather pillows.

ATTEND THE CHILD AT BEDTIME. Give him light suppers and put him to bed early in a dark room. See that his feet are warm, his stomach easy, and his body not overloaded with blankets and quilts; also, see that the nursery is clean and freshly aired. He will not grow better in a glare of artificial light any more than will your camellias and azaleas.

MAKE CLOTHES FOR SLEEPING. Children should not wear the same garment next to the skin at night which they have worn through the day. If the nightgown is worn more than one night without going to the wash room, it should be hung up to be thoroughly aired during the day, if possible in the sun.

PRAY WITH THEM. Pray with the child in simple and earnest language he can understand. The following beautiful little prayer is said to have been composed and used by a boy 13 years old:

Father, now the day is past, on thy child thy blessing cast;
Near my pillow hand in hand, keep thy guardian angel band;
And throughout the darkling night, bless me with a cheerful light.
Let me rise at morn again, free from every care and pain;
Pressing through life's thorny way, keep me, Father, day by day.

—*The Ladies' Repository,* June 1865

SOOTHE THE CHILD WHO CANNOT SLEEP. Nervous children who toss and turn and cry out that they cannot go to sleep may sometimes be quieted by having their feet rubbed vigorously with a flesh brush. A warm bath will sometimes be effectual, but generally it does not conduce to quiet so much as waken. After adjusting the physical appliances which tend to sleep, tell him to picture himself a little winding brook off in the deep woods carrying upon it a leaf or a chip.

LET THEM WAKE OF THEMSELVES. Never wake up young children of a morning; it is a barbarity.

Rules for Their Diets

The quality of food intended for little children should be carefully studied, as the firmness of their flesh and the hardness of their bones is so dependent upon it.

LET NUTRITION, VARIETY, AND TIME OF YEAR GUIDE SELECTIONS. Every care must be taken to supply children with a variety and abundance of nutritious and digestible food, in which fruit, the cereals, vegetables, milk, mutton, beef, and poultry should be included together with simple sweets and plain puddings chiefly composed of milk, eggs, and flour or bread.

FEED THEIR HUNGER. When children get hungry more often than the occurrence of the regular family meals, they should be supplied with a light repast of digestible character. If a child is hungry, it cannot be well or happy.

DON'T FORGET MILK. Wherever milk is used plentifully, there the children grow into robust men and women; wherever the place is usurped by tea, we have degeneracy, swift and certain.

SERVE THEIR MEALS THUS:

    ❋ The breakfast should be early and plentiful.

    ❋ Mid-day dinners should be varied and always hot—indeed, all food is most digestible when warm—and composed of some plain meat dish, at least two vegetables, and a simple pudding. Soup is invaluable for children, but it must be plain.

    ❋ The supper, given about two hours before retiring, should be light and nutritious and may include warm bread, any form of porridge and milk, custard, simple stewed fruits, and either cool water or cocoa.

Particular Rules for Feeding Little Ones under Three

These outlines will serve to guard those having the care of children from making the mistakes which too often entail a life of weakness or suffering as the consequence equally of injudicious indulgence and of neglect of the most ordinary rules of health.

LIMIT HIS FARE. Grant him novel food sparingly and with discretion as to kind. His stomach is too delicate an organ to be tampered with. Let milk—scalded or boiled, as a rule—be the staple, mixed with farina, barley, or something of the sort. Let him munch Graham bread and light crackers freely. Remove far from him hot bread and griddle cakes.

KEEP WATCH OVER THE COOKING. Unless you have a nurse whom you know for yourself to be faithful and experienced, always superintend the cooking of your baby's food.

SUPPLY PLENTY OF BREAD. Children who have cut all their teeth will thrive well and grow strong if they eat heartily of good bread every day. Homemade bread should be eaten in preference to baker's bread, because in baker's bread some of those valuable nutritive parts are destroyed, and while it satisfies hunger, it does not nourish the body.

What Can One Do with Such Chaos?

Her baby was ill and she sent a big boy running for me. "Mam wants you to come right away—the baby's in a fit." Luckily a hot bath put it right. She was quite silent and impassive as I bathed and rubbed the struggling little thing and only spoke after nausea had relieved it of a long slip of salt pork, and left it again comfortable: "Well, you air smart. Your boys look so hearty I thought you'd know all about fits." She laughed to scorn my saying a baby not a year old could not manage solid food, and pointed to her little crowd—huddled around us, watching: "They always eat everything I did, coffee and pork and everything, and I never buried one!" What can one do with such chaos?

Jessie Benton Freemont, *Far-West Sketches*, 1890

GIVE TO HIM THESE FOODS:

- ❈ Mealy old potatoes—never new or waxy ones.
- ❈ Young onions, boiled in two waters.
- ❈ Fresh asparagus, green peas, and dry sweet potatoes should suffice for vegetables.
- ❈ Rice and hominy, of course.

Nursing women should not give way to temper. Anger, anxiety, suspense, fear, terror, and undue conditions of any kind will turn the milk to poison.

Gradual weaning is much better than the sudden removal of the child from the breast. ... A child should not be weaned in the hot months.

—*Sloan's Cook Book and Advice to Housekeepers,* 1905

GIVE HIM THESE, ONCE IN A WHILE, FOR DESSERT:

- ❉ A simple custard.
- ❉ A taste of homemade ice cream, rice, and farina puddings.
- ❉ Graham hasty pudding.
- ❉ The inner part of a well-roasted apple.
- ❉ In their season, ripe peaches.

MOTHER, PROTECT HIM. Hundreds of infants have been killed by parents in giving them improper foods; thus, take care to avoid:

- ☙ Food prepared for other members of the family, as the table foods may be poisonous to the infant.
- ☙ Skin of an apple, which is as bad for him as a bit of your kid gloves would be; and the skin of a grape, more indigestible than sole leather.
- ☙ Raisins—skins and all—which are unfit for anybody to eat and poisonous for a baby.

NEVER GIVE A CHILD UNDER TWO YEARS OF AGE THESE FOODS:

- ☙ Ham, bacon, or pork in any other form.
- ☙ Cabbage, pickles, or other succulent vegetables.
- ☙ Coffee, tea, beer, wine, cider, or any other alcoholic liquor.
- ☙ Bananas, berries, or other fruit except prune juice.
- ☙ Pastries or preserves.

Recipes for the Nursery

Some of the finest children I have seen were reared upon this diet.

CONDENSED MILK. This is perhaps the safest substitute for the "good milk from one cow," which few mothers in town can procure. Keep the can in a cool place and mix according to its directions.

FARINA. Stir 1 large tablespoonful Hecker's Farina, wet up with cold water, into 1 cup boiling water (slightly salted) in the farina kettle (i.e, one boiler set within another, the latter filled with hot water). Boil 15 minutes, stirring constantly until it is well thickened. Then add 1 cup fresh milk, stirring in gradually, and boil 15 minutes longer. Sweeten with 2 teaspoonsful white sugar and give to the child as soon as it is cool enough. You may make enough in the morning to last all day; warming it up with a little hot milk as you want it. Keep it in a cold place, do not get it too sweet, and cook it well.

ARROWROOT. Stir arrowroot paste of 2 teaspoonsful best Bermuda arrowroot, wet with cold water, into 1 cup boiling water with one small pinch of salt; stir and boil 5 minutes or until it is clear; add 2 even teaspoonsful white sugar, dissolved in 1 cup fresh milk. Boil 10 minutes, slowly, still stirring. If the child has fever or cannot digest milk, substitute hot water for it.

MILK AND BREAD. Crumble 2 tablespoonsful stale Graham bread into ½ cup boiled milk, sweeten with a very little sugar; when cool enough, feed to the child with a spoon.

WHEATEN GRITS. Soak 4 tablespoonsful grits (cracked wheat) in a little cold water 1 hour and then put into the kettle. Boil the soaked grits in a quart of water 1 hour, stirring up often; add 1 cup milk and a pinch of salt and boil half an hour longer. Sweeten to taste and, if the child is well, pour cream over it. This is designed for children over a year old.

GRAHAM HASTY PUDDING. Stir 1 cup Graham flour, wet up with cold water, into 1 large cup boiling water with 1 teaspoonful salt. Boil 10 minutes, stirring almost constantly. Add 1 large cup milk and cook, after it has come again to a boil, 10 minutes longer. Give with sugar and milk for breakfast. Eaten with cream, nutmeg, and powdered sugar, this is a good plain dessert for grown people as well as children.

Thoughts on Their Dress (and Yours)

DRESS LITTLE GIRLS WARMLY. On cold, windy days, I am pained to see the efforts of foolish parents to freeze their little girls. It is an outrage. The poor little shivering things are sent out into the streets with their heads comfortably protected and thick shawls around their shoulders, which comparatively need no protection, yet with their skirts standing out at an angle of 45 degrees and their poor little drum-stick legs as unprotected from the blasts as the legs of a turkey hanging in a meat stall.

PROTECT THEIR ARMS AND SHOULDERS. If the mother desires to exhibit her darling's beautiful skin, let her cut out a bit of the dress upon its chest; when the neighbors come in, let her show the skin thus exposed to the company. This skin is so near the furnace of the body it has no chance to get cold; but, in the case of

The reason we admire the tapering waist is because we have been wrongly educated. We have acquired wrong ideas of beauty. We have accepted the ideals of the fashion-plate rather than those of the Creator. We find that some form of physical deformity maintains in almost every country. The Chinese deform the feet, and we think this is barbarous, but it is really not as serious as the deforming of the vital parts of the body.

—*What a Young Woman Ought to Know,* 1898

the arms and legs, the blood has to make a long journey before it can return to the chest for a new supply of warmth. These parts, therefore, need special protection. As cold currents of blood come from both arms back into the vital organs, they play the mischief there. To save a child from croup, pneumonia, and other grave affections, keep her arms warm.

DO NOT CONTRACT THE WAISTS OF YOUR LITTLE GIRLS. Thousands of women are rendered unfit for marriage and motherhood by what they suffer as the result of tight lacing. There are scores of corset-wearing mothers, but point out to me one healthy one out of each score, and I'll show you 19 prematurely wrinkled and wan, fretful, and ailing women to offset your one.

Mercerized cheviot, madras and the new silky-looking French ginghams are made into the most charming summer frocks for girls who are still wearing short skirts. White embroidery, straps and tabs of white linen or pique and even coarse laces are used for trimmings. A dainty little frock of pink and white French gingham has a large bertha of white pique. Another delightful costume is of pale-blue chambray, with a fancy bertha of tucked white lawn and lace.

White stockings are still considered the smart thing for little tots to wear with all sorts of light-colored costumes. Very odd these tiny white legs look coming out beneath the modish black silk coats.

—"Styles of the Month for Children," in *McCall's Magazine,* May 1908

MIND YOUR OWN DRESS FOR THEM. Many a good, kind, loving mother has made her son or her daughter extremely unhappy by appearing not as well dressed, or not as considerate of the ways of the world as her children have a right to expect. We are told in the good book about respect due to our parents, but you and I and the other women have a duty to respect our children, and not to cause them to be mortified by our personal appearance. This may sound a little cruel, but I am sure you will see its truth if you will only remember the times when you have seen your boy's or your girl's face flush because "mother didn't look like the other ladies."

Some Advice for Their Playtime

AMUSE THE BABY SIMPLY:

One mother used to give her baby a wide-mouthed bottle and a box of beans, and he would amuse himself for a long time dropping them one by one into the bottle.

Another amusement for when he was just old enough to stand beside a chair was to give him a lead pencil and let him poke holes through a paper as it lay across a cane-seated chair. A simple device, but it helped the mother "make time," and so the end desired was gained.

LET THEM MAKE THEIR OWN PLAYTHINGS. A little girl had better fashion her cups and saucers of acorns than to have a set of earthen ones supplied. A boy takes ten times more pleasure in a little wooden cart he has pegged together than he would in a painted and gilded carriage bought from the toy shop.

MAKE HER A DOLL. For the wee girl, make a nice rag doll; it will please her as well as a bought one; besides, that sort of dollie can be handled ever so roughly without any danger of breaking its neck or limbs.

April 8, 1867

Today I have been making Vatie's doll a new suit & I have been well paid. She is so pleased & dolly looks so nice in her blue silk dress & saque & white waist.

—Amelia Butts (Mrs. George) Buss, *Diary,* 1866-1867

ENCOURAGE FRIENDSHIPS. Children, to be truly happy, must have the companionship of other children. Unless a child's companions are really objectionable, the evil of no companionship is greater than the risk of letting him play with his mates.

SEND THEM OUT. "All outdoors" is the only proper apartment for children. Nothing can make up for it—for the gleeful delight of picking shells upon the seashore, or paddling with dimpled feet in the foam of the waves, or plucking a handful of flowers wherever one chooses to stray, or looking at the animal creation, every one of which, from a caterpillar to an ox, is a marvel and wonder compared to which a toy shop is of no interest whatever. Such a child is neither fettered by fine clothes nor tyrannized over by a stupid, ignorant, selfish nurse.

Baby outdoors

TAKE YOUR BABY OUT, TOO. A baby can no more flourish in the dark than a flower. Like the flower, it needs sunshine and should have the direct rays from the sun. Do not fear its eyes will be injured if the sun shines on its face; and when you take it out to ride, unless the sun is very strong, do not cover up its face with the carriage top.

GARDEN WITH THEM. Give children a corner "all their own" and some seeds to put in it. Show them how to make beds and take care of them; tell them how flowers grow and encourage them to watch and study them. Such employment will keep them out of a great deal of mischief.

MAKE FUN IN NATURE. Hunting nuts in the real woods is a joy which children should taste more often, for in these days of railroads and electric cars the woods are not so very far off, and once a year at least there should be a nutting party in every well-regulated family.

Threading a Needle

SURELY I think Nurse has forgotten
How hard it is to thread this cotton—
It is so very long ago
Since she was small like me and slow—
Thread, needle, thread, Nurse says I must do it—
Dear Nurse, indeed the cotton won't come through it!

—*Enchanted Tulips and Other Verses for Children,* 1914

Miscellaneous Recipes for Discontented Babies

TO SOOTHE THE TEETHING BABY. For the sleeplessness, irritability, and discomfort which so often accompany teething, much can be done by the mother:

- A hot footbath will often have a soothing effect by relieving the congestion in the head and mouth. Mustard can be added with benefit.

- A good movement of the bowels, induced with castor oil, will relieve congestion in the gums.

- The mother's finger dipped in syrup of lettuce can be gently carried over the tender and inflamed gum and, now and then, by a little firmer pressure, may allow the point of the tooth to free its way.

- Make a dried-flour mixture by tying 1 cup of flour into a stout muslin bag and dropping it into cold water. Then set the bag and water over the fire. Boil three hours steadily. Turn out the flour ball and dry it in the hot sun all day; or, if you need it at once, dry it in a moderate oven without shutting the door. To use it, grate 1 tablespoon for a cup of boiling milk and water (half and half). Wet up the flour with a very little cold water; stir in, and boil five minutes. Put in a little salt.

TO SOOTHE COLICKY BABIES. Paregoric, whiskey, brandy, or soothing syrup are improper remedies for colic. Drugging the baby into insensibility will not cure the cause of illness. Colic is often a symptom of another condition, so this condition must be ascertained and treated thus:

- For colic that may come from cold hands and feet, keep a flannel belly band on the baby in both summer and winter.

- Colic is often due to constipation, in which case an enema of warm water—with the addition of salt at the rate of a level teaspoon to the pint—is required, followed by 1 or 2 teaspoons of castor oil or other gentle laxative medicine.

Whooping Cough Syrup

Make a syrup of prickly pear, a species of cactus, and drink freely. Take about three moderate sized leaves of the prickly pear to a quart of cold water, cut up in pieces and boil slowly about half an hour, strain out all the prickles through close muslin or linen, sweeten with white sugar and boil a little longer. A safe and sure cure, and so pleasant to the taste that infants will take it with a relish. It is also good for a cold that settles in the throat or lungs. This species of cactus grows in rocky and sandy places and is grown in gardens. I should say from a teaspoonful to a tablespoonful for a child, as needed, according to age. For an adult, one to two tablespoonsful.

—*Dr. Chase's Third Last and Complete Receipt Book and Household Physician,* 1903

Miscellaneous Recipes for Sick Children

TO PREVENT CROUP. Take two skeins of black sewing silk, braid them together so they will wear well, and tie the braid loosely around the neck so it is worn below the clothes out of sight; and the child will never have the croup while it is worn. Now, some will laugh at this and call it an old woman's notion, but as it costs but little and can do no harm, if you will only try it, you will save the little ones lots of misery and yourselves many a sleepless night.

TO TREAT CROUP. The instant croupy threatenings are observed, keep the child indoors and serve light food—and not much of that—until the symptoms have abated. Put a mustard plaster on the windpipe, and let it redden the skin but not blister. Put the child's feet in mustard water as hot as they can bear it. Then wipe them dry and keep them covered. Croup requires very prompt treatment; if home treatment does not relieve the child, send immediately for a physician.

TO REMEDY A COUGH OR WHOOPING COUGH:

⊕ Spread butter plentifully on paper (to protect clothing) and lay it over the chest, letting it come well up to the throat.

⊕ Administer a syrup formed from sugar and onion juice.

⊕ Rub the feet thoroughly with hog's lard before the fire, on going to bed—and keep the child warm therein.

⊕ Rub the back, at lying down, with old rum; it seldom fails.

⊕ Give a spoonful of juice of pennyroyal mixed with brown sugar twice a day.

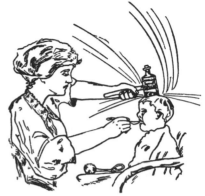

Soothing syrups are poisons to babies. They contain opium. Opium kills babies. Don't dope your baby.

⊕ Give ½ pint of milk, warm from the cow, with the quantity of a nutmeg of conserve of roses dissolved in it, every morning.

⊕ In desperate cases, change of air will have a good effect.

TO RELIEVE A TOOTHACHE. Cut a large raisin open, roast it or heat it, and apply it around the tooth while it is as hot as can be borne. It will operate like a little poultice and will draw out the inflammation.

TO PREVENT RICKETS, TENDERNESS, AND WEAKNESS. Dip children in cold water every morning, at least till they are eight or nine months old. No roller should ever be put round their bodies, nor any stays used. Instead, when they are put into short petticoats, put a waistcoat under their frocks. It is best to wean a child when seven months old, if it be disposed to rickets. It should lie in the cradle at least a year.

Treatment of Jaundice in Children

J. E. Ball, M. D. reports a case as follows:

February 3rd: Called to a child 18 months old; skin and eyes as yellow as saffron, urine thick—stained its clothes that saffron color peculiar to jaundiced urine. Prescribed: Leptandrin, 1 gram; podophyllin, ½ gram; pulverized Jamaica ginger, 2 grams; mixed, and divided into 8 powders. Gave 1 powder every 4 hours until the biliary secretions were aroused. Also Tincture of buchu and sweet spirits of niter, each 1 dram, 10 drops every 2 hours.

February 5th: First prescriptions acted well. Then prescribed: Extract of fringe tree and tincture of blood root, each equal parts, 10 drops 4 times per day.

February 12th: Little patient entirely relieved; skin and urine as clear as it ever was.

—*Dr. Chase's Third Last and Complete Receipt Book and Household Physician*, 1903

Cures the Orphans

The Rev. Mother of the Convent of the Holy Family, Baltic, Conn., can speak very highly of the Kickapoo Indian Remedies. She always has a supply of each kind on hand the year around. For several years they have stood the test in every case. The health of the 200 children under her care is paramount to everything else. A fever, cold, or a cough is seldom known, thanks to the Kickapoo Indian Sagwa, Indian Oil, and Indian Cough Cure; the Kickapoo Indian Salve and Kickapoo Indian Worm Killer have often proved their effectiveness as well.

—*Healy & Bigelow's New Cook Book*, 1890

Chapter Six

---

*F*or the Mother, as Instructress

The Parental Example

If parents realized how great is their responsibility, how closely they are watched, they would place a perpetual guard upon their lips and manners.

BE WHAT YOU WOULD HAVE THEM BECOME. Mother, be what the children ought to be. Do what the children ought to do. Avoid what they should avoid. Know that those by whom you are surrounded are often only reflections of yourself. Are any among them defective? Examine what you are yourself, what you do, what you avoid—in a word, your whole conduct. Do you discover in yourself defects, sins, wandering? Begin by improving yourself and seek afterward to improve your children.

BE HONEST, BE RIGHT. Let there be no deception, no trickery for the keen eye of childhood to detect. Rule your own spirit and wear an unruffled brow, lest the smiling cherub on your knee catch your angry frown. Never stoop to pander with expediency. If a question of right or wrong comes up for decision, meet it squarely. Let your children feel that mother and father are always found on the side of the right.

ASSURE THAT YOUR HUSBAND IS WITH THEM. The father who plunges into business so deeply that he has no leisure for domestic pleasures and whose only intercourse with his children consists in a brief word of authority or a surly lamentation over their intolerable expensiveness is to be both pitied and blamed.

☞

Helen, the eldest daughter, has just come home from school. She is the special, tender delight of her father's eye—pale and delicate in face and physique, clear blue eyes, and auburn hair. . . At the sound of the dinner bell, she slipped quietly into her accustomed place at table, unnoticed by her father, who was not in the secret of her arrival. Soon, in helping round, he came in course to Helen's plate, when he looked up, and lo! such a quick embrace of father and daughter! It was a picture, which only those who have had and have lost such fathers know how to appreciate.

—Celia M. French, "Aunt Sally's Home," in *Ladies' Repository,*
February 1873

The Proper Use of Praise and Punishment

There are two great motives influencing human action—hope and fear. Both of these are at times necessary. But who would not prefer to have her child influenced to good conduct by a desire of pleasing rather than by the fear of offending?

UNDERSTAND AND REASON WITH THEM. The fear of ridicule, pain, and shame drives children into falsehoods. Lies caused by dread of punishment may be avoided if it is understood that a child guilty of a wrong should be forgiven if he made a straightforward, honest acknowledgment of the same. Children are very delicate instruments. Men play upon them as if they were tough as drums and, like drums, made for beating. Do not terrorize them, but reason gently and plainly with them. One in sympathy with their little souls will lead them along safely amid temptations to falsehood.

PRAISE THEM. Parents who never have a word of praise for their children, who deny a bit of approval or a welcoming smile to their own— although they are generous enough with both to strangers—do not know what they are doing. They are chilling the warmest feelings of the heart. They are withering the bright blossoms of love and confidence which cannot live without careful nurture.

PUNISH CONSISTENTLY. Let your punishments be consistent, direct, unhesitating, and not to be escaped; the punishment need not and should not be severe, just enough to let the sensitive heart of the child understand that mother is displeased. I think you will find that, by this method, you reduce the punishment you would otherwise be compelled to inflict, for you soon secure a habit of obedience, after which punishments will be almost unnecessary.

ADMINISTER PUNISHMENT WITH SELF-POSSESSION. If done in a towering passion, punishment takes the character of revenge, and the child resists it with defiance, stubbornness, or a feeling of being the injured party. Place clearly before the child the nature of the aggravation and assure the child that the sole design of the chastisement is his present and future welfare.

PUNISH PRIVATELY. Never correct a child by scolding, admonition, or castigation in public. It is an attack on the child's self esteem, which provokes resistance and arouses a rebellious spirit which often breaks out in open defiance or sullen resentment.

REFRAIN FROM FAULT-FINDING. Scolding, finding fault, and recrimination are below the dignity of punishment. Nothing will rasp and embitter the soul more deeply than a railing, "nagging" tongue. Mothers often fall into the habit of chiding their children for every little offense. It is "Don't do this" and "don't do that," from morning until night. The command becomes odious to the child, and he pays as little attention to his mother's remonstrance as to a cat's meow.

SPEAK GENTLY. I know some houses in which sharp, angry tones resound from morning till night, and the influence is as contagious as measles and much more to be dreaded in a household. The children catch it and it lasts for life—an incurable disease.

What to Teach at Home

There are few who can receive the honors of a college, but all are graduates of the hearth.

CULTIVATE THEIR MENTAL POWERS. Parents have been warned of late that a child with a precocious brain is more liable to dangerous diseases of the brain than other children and that indulging their precocious appetites will increase the excitement of the brain and result in inflammation and premature death. Parents have, therefore, been urged to retard the education of the mental powers, but modern mental science acknowledges that we may begin at a very early period to work upon the conceptive and perceptive faculties, not only without danger, but with manifest advantage.

ALLOW THEM CHOICE OF THEIR OWN OCCUPATIONS. Watch the bent of the young minds; converse with them as to their predilections. They will learn any business more readily if they are interested in it. Let this determine you to leave them unfettered in their choice.

TEACH THEM INDEPENDENCE. All children should cherish a desire to do all they can for themselves and to support themselves by their labor as early as possible. Those who lean on father and mother for everything will find it hard work to get along by and by, as they may have to do when their parents die. Those who early learn to rely upon themselves will have little difficulty in earning their own living.

TEACH DAUGHTERS THE LESSONS OF THE HOME. No matter your daughter's position, in our country of variable fortunes there is no insurance against her compulsion to go into the kitchen for her daily bread once she is a wife. The time may not come when the daughters of wealth shall be obliged to take their stand in the kitchen, but should they not know how to bake and wash? We shall never have good puddings and pies, chowders and fricassees, while the ladies are taught that it is a disgrace to learn to cook. Teach them how to make bread as well as rick-rack. If they show a talent for music, give them a chance, but not before they can broil a steak or make a decent cup of coffee.

TEACH SONS TO EARN THEIR OWN. Many an unwise parent labors hard and lives sparingly for the purpose of giving his children a start in the world, as it is called. Instead of striving to lay up fortunes for your son, teach him the habits of business and so give him treasures more staple than stocks and bonds. Setting a young man afloat with money left by relatives is like tying bladders under the arms of one who cannot swim; ten chances to one he will lose his bladders and go to the bottom. Teach him to swim.

🖙

The family consists of a boy and three girls, all of whom take their share of the house-duties. The girls, amongst other cares, milk some twenty head of cows twice a day, churn the milk, make the butter, assist in the cooking, and attend to the welfare of the poultry and calves. The boy helps his father with the farmwork, collects the milch cows, and is always in readiness to ride anywhere, at his father's commands, on his fleet-footed pony. Work is never slack on such a farm.

—Brendan MacCarthy, "Home Life in Colorado," in *Catholic World,* 1884

Rules for Children's Deportment

It is the practice with certain people to sneer at the word "etiquette" and to claim it merely means a foolish pandering to frivolous customs which in themselves have no meaning or use. This is a misapprehension which a little thoughtful consideration will remove. A knowledge of etiquette may be said to be an important part of good breeding.

OBEDIENCE. The first lesson a child should be taught is filial respect and a deferent yielding of its own wishes to those of its parents. This does not imply a slavish submission or a crushing-out of individuality. It means that the tie between parent and child should be so strong and the confidence so great that there would be no chance for the clashing of will.

COURTESY. Children must not be allowed to have two sets of manners, one for home and one for company. They can be taught to exercise gentle manners at home, to be thoughtful of the comfort of every family member, and to be guilty of no act that they would blush for were other eyes upon them. Then they will become real gentlemen or ladies.

RESPECT FOR OTHERS. Children can be trained to reciprocate courtesies and to behave politely everywhere without making prim little martinets of them. Teach them to respect each other's rights—to enjoy their merry romp and innocent fun without hurting each other's feelings or playing upon some weakness.

RESPECT FOR ELDERS. Teach them to be deferent to their superiors in age and position. "Young America" has the idea that it is a proof of independence to speak flippantly and sneeringly of parents or guardians, referring to them as "the governor," "the old lady," or "the old party." There is no greater mistake made, and the listeners who may smile at such "wit" will just as likely censure for such coarseness and disrespect.

SILENCE. It is very rude for children to ask direct questions, such as "Where are you going?" or "What have you got in that package?" In fact, they should not show curiosity about other people's affairs.

MODESTY. Modesty among boys and girls is as highly appreciated as among grown people; and a young person who thinks himself a little better than his associates can hardly help carrying the thought into action. By such conduct he makes himself exceedingly disagreeable.

MANNERS. Many children form habits which are not nice, such as spitting on the floor, scratching the head, stretching themselves out upon a chair, and yawning. All such habits are exceedingly low bred.

SUCCINCTNESS. If they have occasion to enter a place of business, train your children to state what they want and then retire as quickly as possible. They have no right to encroach upon the time of a businessman.

Teaching Table Manners

Some little folks are not polite at their meals. The following stan-
dards are so simple... we take pleasure in placing them conspicuously
before our readers. They will bear memorizing.

In silence I must take my seat,
And give God thanks before I eat;
Must for my food in patience wait,
Till I am asked to hand my plate;
I must not scold, nor whine, nor pout,
Nor move my chair or plate about;
With knife, or fork, or napkin ring,
I must not play—nor must I sing;
I must not speak a useless word,
For children must be seen—not heard;
I must not talk about my food,
Nor fret if I don't think it good;
My mouth, with food I must not crowd,
Nor while I'm eating speak aloud;
Must turn my head to cough or sneeze,
And when I ask, say, "If you please;"
The tablecloth I must not spoil,
Nor with my food my fingers soil;
I must keep my seat when I am done,
Nor round the table sport or run;
When told to rise, then I must put
My chair away with noiseless foot,
And lift my heart to God above,
In praise for all his wondrous love.

—*The Ladies' Repository,* February 1865

CHAPTER SEVEN

*F*OR THE NURSE

KEEP UP A FIRE. The sight of a bright blaze is calculated to cheer the patient, while the sight of a dark, closed stove is depressing. By no means allow a sick person to be in a room warmed by a flue or register.

KEEP HIM CHEERED. The patient should be indulged in every fancy that is not hurtful. Study all pleasant and soothing arts to while away the time and keep worry of every kind away from him. A trifle at which you can laugh will be a burden to the enfeebled mind and body of a patient who has nothing to do but lie still and roll it over in his mind until it swells into a mountain.

WELCOME THE SUN FOR HIM. Cases are not rare in which invalids have been restored to health by using sunbaths and otherwise freely enjoying the sunshine. The old idea of darkening the sick room is exploded. The modern science of physics has come to recognize sunshine as one of the most powerful of remedial agencies. If the patient's eyes are weak, admit the sunshine from a quarter where it will not fall upon them.

CLEAN WHILE THE PATIENT IS OUT. Let such sweeping and dusting as are necessary be also done with dispatch, using a dust-pan to receive the dust from the carpet. Avoid raising clouds of dust from the carpet, and of ashes from the fireplace. Make arrangements for the patient on returning from a convalescent drive to find the room thoroughly cleaned, aired, and adorned with fresh flowers, and let the bed be nicely made up and turned down.

Few people realize the vast difference that exists between a so-called well-ventilated room and the open air—the former is enough to kill an Indian.

—G.F. Gardiner, *Light and air in the treatment of consumption in Colorado,* 1903

MANAGE ODORS. It is best to have no odors in the sick room unless it be bay rum, German cologne, or something else especially fancied by the sick person. Cologne water will not dispel a foul odor, while disinfectants are noisome. When there is any unpleasant exhalation, it is far better to let is escape by properly ventilating the room than to try to overcome it by the aid of perfumery. In fevers, where there are offensive exhalations from the body, sponging the patient with tepid water will help remove the odor.

Chasing the Cure in Colorado

It is not unusual to see an invalid sitting on a covered porch, overcoated, furred, and blanketed, with hot bricks or a hot water bag at his feet. Meanwhile, snow is swirling and drifting over him, and the thermometer is not far above zero... When he reaches for the glass of water by his side... it is frozen hard.

—T.C. Galbreath, *Chasing the Cure in Colorado,* 1908

MIND HIS SENSITIVITIES. Do not keep the medicines where he can see them, nor ever let him witness the mixing of that which he is to swallow. As soon as his meals are over, remove every vestige of them from the room. Even a soiled spoon, lying on table or bureau, may offend his fastidious appetite. Cover the stand or waiter from which he eats with a spotless napkin, and serve his food in your daintiest ware.

ARRANGE A DRIVE. Driving is a delightful recreation for convalescents; they should be indulged in it as soon as the physician pronounces it safe. In winter, they should be carried driving about noon so as to enjoy the sunshine at its warmest. In summer, the cool of the morning or evening is the best time to drive them out, but be careful to return immediately after sundown. It is well to have some little refreshment awaiting the patient after a drive—a little cream or milk toddy, a cup of tea or coffee, or, if the weather be hot, some cooling draught perhaps would be more acceptable.

☛ *Hospital Nurses, Take Heed* ☚

Once admitted, a patient is forbidden to use any profane or indecent language, to express immoral sentiments, to play at any game for money, to use intoxicating liquors, to have any literature of immoral or indecent nature, to use tobacco, or to spit upon the floor of the wards, hall, or stairways, nor out of the windows.

*—Constitution, By-laws and House Rules of the Citizen's
Hospital Association of Pitkin County, 1892*

DO NOT ADMIT VISITORS. In a case of illness, many well-meaning persons crowd to see the patient. Do not admit them into the sick room, as it is too exciting and fatiguing to an ill person to see company; and, when in a critical condition, the balance might be disastrously turned by the injudicious admission of visitors.

Miscellaneous Recipes for Ailing Adults

To REMEDY ALMOST ANYTHING. Break an egg. Separate the yolk and white. Whip each to a stiff froth. Add 1 tablespoonful of arrowroot and a little water to the yolk. Rub till smooth and free from lumps. Pour slowly into a ½ pint of boiling water, stirring all the time. Let it simmer till jelly-like. Sweeten to the taste and add 1 tablespoonful of French brandy. Stir in the frothed white and take hot in winter. In summer, set first on ice, then stir in the beaten white. Milk may be used instead of water.

To CURE THE HEART OF AN ACHE. Take a piece of the lean of mutton, about the size of a large walnut, put it into the fire and burn it till it becomes reduced to a cinder, then put it into a clean rag and squeeze it until some moisture is expressed, which must be dropped in the ear as hot as the patient can bear.

To TREAT ACUTE CARDIAC PAIN. Whether or not the pain is due to angina pectoris, a mustard plaster will relieve you.

Coloradians are the most disappointed people I ever saw. Two-thirds of them came here to die, and they can't do it. This wonderful air brings them back from the very edge of the tomb, and they are naturally exceedingly disappointed.

—P. T. Barnum, ca. 1872

To CURE THOSE ADDICTED TO DRINKING WINE. Put in a sufficient quantity of wine 3 or 4 large eels, and leave there till quite dead. Give that wine to the person you want to reform, and he or she will be so much disgusted with wine, that though they formerly made use of it, they will now have an aversion to it.

To TREAT A BURN OR SCALD. Cover it with wet linen cloths, pouring on more water without removing them till the pain is alleviated, when pure hog's lard may be applied. Or apply lather of soap from the shaving cup with the brush to produce relief. White of egg applied in the same way is also a simple and useful dressing. If the shock is great and there is no reaction, administer frequently aromatic of ammonia or a little brandy and water till the patient rallies.

Protecting from Colorado's Sun

The sympathetic chambermaid of the Beebee House had been hovering in my doorway for a half hour before the start, urging me to take more and more wraps, and relating horrible anecdotes of the Chicago lady 'who had her nose burned to a white blister and her face so raw, ma'am, that we could hardly touch it with a feather for three days.' With such gentle admonition there was no struggle when the kindhearted one proceeded to apply her preventive, and under a triple layer of cold cream powder and barege veils we made the trip and returned rather fairer in skin for the bleaching process.

—Ernest Ingersoll, *The Crest of the Continent: A Summer's Ramble in the Rocky Mountains and Beyond,* 1885

TO BIND A CUT. Dissolve ocean salt in a pitcher of water and rub this on the flesh with a sponge; or apply cobwebs and brown sugar or the dust of tea, applied with laudanum.

TO TREAT VENOMOUS BITES. Apply a moderately tight ligature above the bite. Wash the wound freely with water to encourage bleeding, then cauterize thoroughly. Afterwards, apply lint dipped in equal parts of olive oil and spirits hartshorn; swallow 10 drops dissolved in a wineglass of water.

TO CURE A TOOTHACHE. Saturate a piece of wool with a mixture of 6 grains morphia and a ½ ounce each of tincture of aconite root, chloroform, laudrum, creosote, oil cloves, and cajuput; add as much gum camphor as the chloroform will dissolve. Put it in the hollow tooth, being certain that the cavity is cleaned out. Catnip leaves are also reputed beneficial for a toothache when masticated and applied to the decayed tooth.

TO CURE A HEADACHE. The fresh juice of ground ivy snuffed up the nose; ginger powder, formed into a plaster with warm water and applied on paper or cloth to the forehead; a mustard poultice applied to the nape of the neck; or a footbath, taken for the purpose of drawing the blood from the head, can all relieve aching of the head.

TO RELIEVE TESTICULAR PAIN.
The constant use of an elm bark poultice, regularly changed every four hours, will be found a superior remedy for the excruciating pains of the testes which accompany the metastasis of mumps, whether of recent or long standing.

TO ALLAY NAUSEA. Cloves may be used to allay vomiting and sickness at stomach, to stimulate the digestive functions, improve the flavor or operation of other remedies, and prevent a tendency toward digestion producing sickness or griping.

TO RELIEVE DYSENTERY. Steep black or green tea in boiling water and sweeten with loaf sugar.

Healing Springs (Manitou)

These springs have from time immemorial enjoyed a reputation of healing waters among the Indians. ... During the seasons that the use of these waters has been under observation, it has been noticed that rheumatism, certain skin diseases, and cases of debility have been much benefited, so far confirming the experience of the past. The Manitou and Navajo have also been highly praised for their relief of old kidney and liver troubles, and the Iron Ute for chronic alcoholism and uterine derangements. Many of the phthisical patients who come to this dry, bracing air in increasing numbers are also said to have drunk of the waters with evident advantage.

—Ernest Ingersoll, *The Crest of the Continent: A Summer's Ramble in the Rocky Mountains and Beyond,* 1885

To RELIEVE CONSTIPATION. Castor oil is frequently used to remove constipation. One part oil of turpentine mixed with 3 or 4 parts castor oil increases its purgative effect. The greatest objections to this cathartic are its nauseous taste and tendency to cause sickness or unconquerable disgust. This may be overcome by adding to 1 pint of the oil 1 ounce of sassafras oil; the dose of this may be given in sweetened water. Any other aromatic oils will answer equally as well. When not contraindicated, the oil may be taken in wine, spirituous liquors, or the froth of beer, likewise in cinnamon or peppermint water.

To PREVENT DYSPEPSIA. In most countries, people who indulge in alcoholic drinks take them at meal times or immediately after eating, when the membranous lining of the stomach is in some degree protected from their inflammatory action by a poultice, so to speak, of masticated food. The American imbiber prefers to swallow liquid poison when there is nothing in the organ into which he decants it to qualify its fiery principle or prevent it from taking immediate and full effect upon the viscera with which it comes in contact. Is it any wonder, then, considering the outrages the people of this country commit upon their internal machinery, that dyspepsia is a "national disease"? Take alcohol with your food and not alone.

To remedy dyspepsia:

❧ *Before breakfast.* Rise early, dress warm, and go out. If strong, walk; if weak, saunter. After half an hour or more, come in for breakfast. Drink cold water three times. Of all cold baths, a morning bath is best for the dyspeptic.

❧ *Breakfast.* For breakfast, eat a piece of good steak half as large as your hand, a slice of coarse bread, and a baked apple; eat very slowly. Avoid hot biscuits and strong coffee, and drink nothing. Talk very pleasantly with your neighbors; read cheerful comments of journals.

❧ *Work out of doors.* Digest for an hour, and then to your work; I trust it is in the open air. Work hard till noon, and then rest body and mind till dinner; sleep a little and drink water.

❧ *Dinner.* For dinner at two or three o'clock, eat a slice of beef, mutton, or fish as large as your hand, a potato, two or three spoons of other vegetables, and a slice of coarse bread; give more than half an hour to this meal, and use no drink.

❧ *After dinner.* After dinner, play anaconda poker for an hour.

☛ *Colorado as Sanitorium*

The curative effect of the climate of Colorado can hardly be exaggerated… Colorado is the most remarkable sanitorium in the world… consumptives, asthmatics, dyspeptics, and sufferers from nervous diseases,… here in hundreds and thousands, either trying the "camp cure" for three or four months or settling here permanently. All have come for health, and most have found or are finding it.

—Isabella L. Bird, *A Lady's Life in the Rocky Mountains,* 1881

[76]

❁ *Supper.* Forgo it. Even a little tea and toast will slow your recovery.

❁ *Bedtime routine.* In a warm room, bathe your skin with cold water hastily; go to bed in a well-ventilated room before nine o'clock. Follow this prescription for three months, and your stomach will so far recover that you can indulge for some time in all sorts of irregular and gluttonous eating. Or if you have resolved, in the fear of Heaven, to present your body a living sacrifice, holy and acceptable unto God, then continue to eat and work like a Christian, and your distressing malady will soon be forgotten.

To RELIEVE COUGHS. Boil 1 ounce licorice root in ½ pint of water till it is reduced by half. Then add 1 ounce gum arabic and 1 ounce loaf sugar. Take 1 teaspoonful every few hours. Or, boil 3 lemons for 15 minutes. Slice them thin while hot over 1 pound of loaf sugar. Put on the fire in a porcelain-lined saucepan and stew till the syrup is thick. After taking it from the fire, add 1 tablespoonful oil of sweet almonds. Stir till thoroughly mixed and cool. Take 1 spoonful or more when the cough is troublesome.

To PREVENT COLDS. Many a cold, cough, and consumption are excited into action by pulling off the hat and overcoat by men, and bonnet and shawl by women, immediately on entering the house in winter after a walk. An interval of at least five or ten minutes should be allowed.

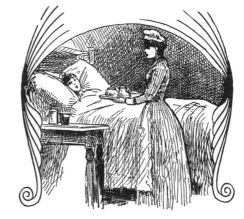

Insert feet in a hot footbath of 3 or 4 tablespoonsful powdered mustard, removing them when the skin reddens and begins to smart. This is also useful in the early stages of colds to induce perspiration.

The Tongue—What It Tells

If ever I was so far left to myself as to meditate some rash act, I should first have a look at my tongue. If it was not perfectly clean and moist I should not consider myself perfectly healthy, nor perfectly sane, and would postpone my proceedings in the hope that my worldly prospects would get brighter. The tongue sympathizes with every trifling ailment of body or mind, and more especially with the state of the stomach. I sincerely believe that real comfort cannot be secured in this world by any one who does not keep his feet warm, his head cool, and his tongue clean.

—Dr. Chase's Third Last and
Complete Receipt Book and
Household Physician, 1903

Other Conditions and Cures

Other substances with the ability to heal various conditions:

🖎   *Ginger* is eminently useful in habitual flatulency, atonic dyspepsia, hysteria, and enfeebled and relaxed habits, especially of old and gouty individuals. Ginger, in the form of "ginger tea," is also popular and efficient in relieving the pangs of disordered menstruation.

🖎   *Ivy leaves* in the form of decoction applied locally have been efficient in treating diseases of the skin, indolent ulcers, eczemas, and itch; this will also destroy vermin in the hair, which, it should be stated, is stained black by the application.

🖎   *Parsley seeds,* as well as the leaves, sprinkled on the hair in powder or in the form of an ointment, will destroy vermin.

🖎   *Mistletoe* is asserted to be of some value in restraining postpartum hemorrhages. It has also been beneficially employed in epilepsy, hysteria, insanity, paralysis, and other nervous diseases. In using this agent, it is always necessary to regulate the condition of the stomach and bowels, the menstrual discharge and other faulty secretions, and remove worms, if any are present, previous to its exhibition.

🌿 *Sage* is a valuable anaphrodisiac to check excessive venereal desires. It may be used in connection with moral, hygienic, and other aids, if necessary.

🌿 *Vanilla* is an aromatic stimulant said to exhilarate the brain, prevent sleep, increase muscular energy, and stimulate the sexual propensities. It is also considered an aphrodisiac, powerfully exciting the generative system and much used in perfumery and to flavor tinctures, syrups, ointments, and confectionery.

🌿 *Mashed raw onions* applied to the soles of the feet will break up an ache-all-over cold, bid fever depart, and often effect a complete cure in a few hours. Family physicians have reported cases of typhoid fever, typhoid pneumonia, scarlet fever, and diphtheria cured by the use of this poultice unless the patient is very near death.

🌿 The juice of the *orange* has a direct beneficial medicinal influence in all fevers.

🌿 *Nutmeg* is also recommended for the cure of fever. Char a nutmeg by holding it to the flame and permitting it to burn by itself without disturbance; when charred, pulverize it,

☛ *Cure for Consumption*

Eat all that the appetite requires of the most nourishing food, such as fresh beef, lambs, oysters, raw eggs, fruits, vegetables, and three times a day take a glass of eggnog, made as rich as the patient can bear; avoid all alcoholic drinks. Bathe twice a week in water made agreeably warm and in a warm room; after bathing, rub the body and limbs with sweet cream or sweet oil. Exercise daily in the open air; walking is the best. Stand erect; exercise the arms and lungs freely, keep the mind cheerful; take freely of the best cough syrup, and consumption will be a stranger to your household.

—*Darley Family Papers*, 186?

To Relieve Coughs

Take 1 ounce of thoroughwort, 1 ounce of slippery elm, 1 ounce stick liquorice, and 1 ounce of flaxseed; simmer together in 1 quart of water until the strength is entirely extracted. A few doses of 1 tablespoonful at a time will alleviate the most distressing cough of the lungs, soothes and allays irritation, and if continued subdues any tendency to consumption; breaks up entirely the whooping cough, and no better remedy can be found for croup asthma, bronchitis, and all affections of the lungs and throat. Thousands of precious lives are saved every year by this cheap and simple remedy as well as thousands of dollars, which would be otherwise spent on the purchase of nostrums, which are both useless and dangerous.

—*Darley Family Papers,* 186?

combine it with an equal quantity of burnt alum, and divide the mixture into three powders. On the commencement of the chill, give a powder. If this does not break it, give the second powder on the approach of the next chill; and if not cured, the third powder must be given as the succeeding chill comes on.

Passionflower is very useful to allay restlessness and overcome wakefulness when these are the result of exhaustion or the nervous excitement of debility. It proves especially useful in the insomnia of infants and old people. The sleep induced by passiflora, as it is known, is a peaceful, restful slumber, and the patient awakens quiet and refreshed.

Rattlesnake Bite

Kill a chicken by cutting off the head at the breast. Place chicken breast over snakebite until venom is drawn out, 30 minutes to 1 hour.

—John Thomas, *Southeast Colorado Rattlesnake Country,*
in *Thomas-Brunelli Family Papers*

❧ Cures of Denver's St. Mark's Ladies Aid Society ❧

TO CURE CHILBLAINS
Soak feet for 15 minutes in warm water, put on a pair of rubbers without stockings, and go to bed.

FOR HOARSENSS
Squeeze the juice of half a lemon in a pint bowl, add loaf sugar (2 tablespoonsful), 1 teaspoonful of glycerine, and 1 tablespoonful of whiskey; pour over this boiling hot water to nearly fill the bowl, and drink hot just before going to bed.

ANTIDOTES TO POISON
For any poison swallow instantly a glass of cold water with a helping teaspoonful of common salt and 1 of ground mustard stirred in. This is a speedy emetic. When it has acted, swallow the whites of 2 raw eggs.

—Our Kitchen Friend, 1889

❧ Cures of Denver Quakers ❧

NERVOUS PROSTRATION
Onions… are almost the best nervine known (and) there is nothing else that will so quickly relieve and tone up a worn-out system.

RINGWORM
Smoke a fine Cuban cigar and take one-half inch of ash. Wet the skin with saliva and rub the ashes in thoroughly; do this three times each day and in a week all will be smooth and well.

—Denver Quaker Cook Book, 1905

Miscelleanous Recipes Just for Females

To FACILITATE CHILDBIRTH. Some physicians consider drinking a ½ pint of elm bark powder boiled in 1 pint of new milk daily, during and after the seventh month of gestation, as advantageous in facilitating and causing an easy delivery.

To CURE CHAPS IN WOMEN'S NIPPLES. Apply balsam of sugar. Or, apply butter of wax, which speedily heals them.

☞ *Fertility*

I have used the Vegetable Compound and it certainly did wonders for me. I was married four years and had great love for children and was really discouraged because I didn't have any. At this time I had a very troublesome complaint and someone told me to take Lydia E. Pinkhams' Vegetable Compound and it sure would help me. In a year I had the sweetest little baby girl who weight 8 ½ pounds. She is now three years old and I have a son two years old. So now I believe in the old saying, 'There's a baby in every bottle.'

—Ms. Mike Rennes,
Fruits and Candies, ca. 1900

To SOFTEN HARD BREASTS. Apply turnips, roasted till soft then mashed and mixed with a little oil of roses. Change this twice a day, keeping the breast very warm with flannel.

To RELIEVE SORE AND SWELLED BREASTS. Boil a handful of chamomile, and as much mallows in milk and water. Foment with it between two flannels, as hot as can be borne, every 12 hours. It also dissolves any knot or swelling in any part where there is no inflammation.

Abortion May Be Caused By

☞ External violence, such as kicks and blows or a fall, or violent action, such as dancing, riding, or jumping. Women in the state of pregnancy should avoid many of the domestic operations so proper at other times for good housewives to engage in. We venture, at the risk of exciting a smile, to mention some exertions that ought to be avoided, viz., hanging up curtains, bedmaking, washing, pushing in a drawer with the foot, careless walking up or down a stair.

☞ Straining of the body, as from coughing.

☞ Costiveness.

☞ Irritation of the neighboring parts, as from severe purging, falling down of the gut, or piles.

☞ Any sudden or strong emotion of the mind, such as fear, joy, or surprise.

☞ The pulling of a tooth; though toothache is occasionally very troublesome to women in the pregnant state, the operation of drawing teeth should, if possible, be avoided at that time.

☞ Marrying when rather advanced in age. It would be hazardous to name any particular age at which it is too late to marry, but the general observation is worth attending to.

☞ Constitutional debility from large evacuations, such as bleeding or purging, or from disease such as dropsy, fever, or smallpox.

☞ A robust and vigorous habit with great fullness of blood and activity of the vascular system.

☞ The death of the child.

—Dr. Chase's Third Last and Complete
Receipt Book and Household Physician, 1903

Women usually deliver lying on the left side, with the knees drawn up towards the abdomen. The right side of the bed, therefore, is the one which requires preparing, and that part of it near the foot is preferable because the upper part of the bed is thus kept clean and comfortable for the patient when the labor is over, and because of the help derived from being able to plant the feet firmly against the bed-post during the pains.

☞ Two pillows are to be put in the center of the bed, so that the patient may lie with the upper part of the body directly across the bed, the hips being as near the edge as possible.

☞ As labor advances and it becomes necessary for the patient to be placed in bed, she should put on a clean chemise and night-dress. Amongst the working classes it is still too much the custom for women to be confined in their everyday dress. It is a practice that ought always to be discountenanced.

☞ The hair should be dressed in such a way that the continuous lying in bed after the confinement will not drag upon or entangle it more than is inevitable.

☞ It is very undesirable for a woman in labor to be surrounded by a number of friends and neighbors.

☞ No nurse should ever allow herself to be teased into prophesying that the labor will be over by a certain hour. If such prophesies turn out incorrect, as they are most likely to do, the patient loses courage and confidence.

☞ All gossip is to be avoided, and nurses should be particularly careful to make no reference to their past experiences, especially such as have been unfavorable. A good, kind nurse will not be at a loss for a few helpful and encouraging words as labor goes on and will not need to have recourse either to foolish promises or dismal anecdotes.

—*Dr. Chase's Third Last and Complete Receipt Book and Household Physician*, 1903

CHAPTER EIGHT

---

*F*OR THE HOMEMAKER SETTING UP HOUSEHOLD

Furnishing and Decorating the Home

The greatest part of our life is spent indoors, and the surroundings and decorations of our particular abode tend to make our existence either more pleasant or unpleasant, either sober or mirthful in countenance.

KNOW THE RESULTS OF YOUR SELECTIONS. Furniture, decorations, and other surroundings that are disorderly or in bad taste have a harmful effect on the character of the inmates of a house. The worst effect is upon the impressionable children, who take their own homes as models; what they see in childhood tends to fix their standards for life. Hence, neat, tasteful, and orderly homes have a very important educational influence.

MODEL TASTE AFTER NATURE. Follow nature and good taste will not be offended. Do not encourage shams; let everything be genuine. Do not substitute the grotesque for the graceful or make a sacrifice of comfort to carry out an idea. Do not paint wood to imitate bronze or plaster to look like stone. Remember that there is an eternal fitness in things. Comfort and taste can easily be combined.

KEEP YOUR HOME IN ORDER. To beautify a home and then freely use it is a duty we owe to that innate love of beauty which God has implanted in us:

- Adorn your house with books, pictures, papers, and enliven it with music.
- Plant trees for shade and trees for fruit; cultivate flowers and shrubbery.
- Keep up the fences.
- Keep the house painted.
- If a gate hinge or a door knob be broken or out of order, repair it at once; let nothing "go to rack."

There is no folly in it, but the best wisdom. Your life will be happier and doubtless longer; and your children will grow up more refined and contented, cherishing a stronger affection for you and an attachment to the home which will make them cling to it and to you when old age comes on.

The knowledge that will enable a young woman to make good bread, cook foods, keep her house in a neat and orderly condition, feed a baby without poisoning it... is of far greater value than a knowledge of Greek, Wagnerian music, or any number of (similar) accomplishments could be.

—E. Stuver, M.D.
Fort Collins, 1902

Colorado Springs, November 1871

*Here I am 'located' at last, and the best thing I can do is to de-
scribe our arrival here, and my first impressions, which, to say the
least, are novel…The streets and blocks are only marked out by a fur-
row turned with the plough, and indicated faintly by a wooden
house, finished, or in process of building, here and there, scattered
over half a mile of prairie. About twelve houses and shanties are in-
habited, most of them unfinished, or run up for temporary occupation; and there are several tents dotted about also. My house is a
wooden shanty, 16 feet by 12, with a door in front, and a small window on each side—they are glass, though they do not open. It is lined
with brown paper, so it is perfectly wind-proof, and really quite
comfortable, though it was ordered on Thursday and finished on Saturday. M. has now put his tent up over the front of the shanty, with
a rough board floor, and it serves for our sitting-room by day and his
bedroom at night; so we can warm both tent and room with a stove
in the former…In the corner by the stove stands a pail of water; and
over it hangs an invaluable tin dipper, which serves for saucepan,
glass, jug, cup, and every use imaginable.*

*I locked myself into my strange new abode, with M.'s revolver as
protection against imaginary foes; and by dint of buffalo-robes and
blankets, and heaps of flannel, managed to keep tolerably warm,
though my breath condensed on the sheets, and when I got up the
bucket had a quarter of an inch of ice on it.*

*—South by West or Winter in the Rocky Mountains
and Spring in Mexico,* 1874

Denver

For many blocks in the southern and western quarter of the town—from Fourteenth to Thirthieth streets, and from Arapahoe to Broadway and the new suburbs beyond—you will see only elegant and comfortable houses. Homes succeed one another in endlessly varying styles of architecture, and vie in attractiveness, each surrounded by lawns and gardens abounding in flowers. All look new and ornate, while some of the dwellings of wealthy citizens are palatial in size and furnishing, and with porches well occupied during the long, cool twilight characteristic of the summer evening in this climate, giving a very attractive air of opulence and ease.

—Ernest Ingersoll, *The Crest of the Continent:*
A Summer's Ramble in the Rocky Mountains and Beyond, 1885

The ranch of my friend Mr. Sutcliffe is situated some ten miles from the county town of Castleton, in Colorado, and is a good example of all that a Western home might be. A glance round the house will make it clear that here comfort and cleanliness reign supreme.

—Brendan MacCarthy, "Home-Life in Colorado," in *Catholic World,* December 1884

The Front Room

SELECT THE ROOM WITH CARE. Let the front part of the house be thrown open and the most convenient room in it be selected as the family room. Let its doors be ever open; when the work of the kitchen is completed, let mother and daughters be found there with their work. Even if the family living room be plain, the children leave traces of their growing up in it, and the faces of the old people who have there lived out their lives look down from its walls.

DRESS APPROPRIATELY. Let no hat ever be seen in that room on the head of its owner; let no coatless individual be permitted to enter it. If father's head is bald his daughter will be proud to see his temples covered by the neat and graceful silken cap that her hands have fashioned for him. If the coat he wears by day is too heavy for the evening, calicoes are cheap and so is cotton wadding. And if his boots are hard and the nails cut mother's carpet, a bushel of wheat once in three years will keep him in slippers of the easiest kind.

 February 9, 1867

This morning George finished our privy. I have not been in to one since the last August & I can't tell you how pleased I feel with it. It is built of logs & has a dirt roof. The seat is good & so is the door.

Amelia Butts (Mrs. George) Buss,
Diary, 1866-1867

OUTFIT THE ROOM WITH A READING AREA. Let that table, which has always stood under the looking glass, against the wall, be wheeled into the room, its leaves raised, and plenty of useful—not ornamental—books and periodicals be laid upon it. When evening comes bring on the lights, and plenty of them, for sons and daughters, all who can, will be most willing students. They will read; they will learn; they will discuss the subjects of their studies with each other; and parents will often be quite as much instructed as their children.

DECORATE THE ROCKING CHAIR. The ugly back of a splint rocking chair can be improved by covering it with a strip of drab linen with a narrow border in outline stitch on each edge. Slip one end between the strips of wood at the top and bring the other end under at the bottom and fasten them securely. They may be kept in place by tying them to the rounds at the top; if done with ribbons this looks pretty.

DECORATE THE WALLS EASILY. The cover designs and full-page illustrations of several of the leading monthlies and other periodicals are reproductions of the best works of prominent artists and illustrators. These are freely used in many homes to decorate the walls of libraries, dens, and sometimes living rooms, either framed or bound in passe-partout binding or merely neatly trimmed with a straight-edge and attached to the wall by means of brass-headed tacks or thumb tacks. A series of cover designs of one or more periodicals makes a very interesting and attractive frieze for the den or library.

CONSIDER CALLERS WHEN TIDYING. As a last finishing touch to the rearranging of the parlor, leave late papers, magazines, a volume of poetry, or a stereoscope and views where they will be readily picked up by callers.

The Dining Room

Of all rooms in the house, the dining room should be the cheeriest, because it is there that all members of the family are most likely to congregate. No matter how widely the interests and occupations of father, mother, and children may separate them at other times of the day, at least one-fifth of their waking hours will probably be spent at the table.

FIT THE ROOM WITH THESE ITEMS.

🕮 *Table.* The table should be firm and solid and not so shaky that the guests fear some catastrophe. Decidedly, square and round tables are the most desirable; because, placed in a circle or nearly facing the host, no guest is given precedence except those who occupy the seats of honor at the right hand of the host and hostess respectively.

🕮 *Chairs.* Chairs upholstered with leather are the nicest, and oak chairs with high backs are popular. Chairs can be made absolutely comfortable with practicable cushions; small hassocks can be placed under the table for additional comfort. Cane-seat chairs should never be used in the dining room; they catch beads and fringes and play havoc with them. The perforated wood ones are equally bad; the brass-headed nails with which they are fastened catch worse

The parlor, on the right of the entrance, is a large room, well lighted with three windows. There is a large, open fireplace, and on winter's nights, when the red curtains aredrawn close and the pitch-pine fire roars up the chimney, you may sit in warm slippers before the cheerful blaze and have only an increased feeling of comfort from the thought that Jack Frost is squeezing the mercury into the bulb of the thermometer outside or screaming enviously round the corners of the house. At the back is a cosey little room devoted to the ladies of the family. Here, amongst other things, are a piano and a sewing machine, and in the long evenings work and music go merrily together. The hall is adorned with a magnificent pair of antlers, a trophy from one of Mr. Sutcliffe's hunting expeditions."

—Brendan MacCarthy, "Home Life in Colorado," in *Catholic World,* 1884

than the cane, and many a delicate fabric has been ruined by them.

Serving Tables. A side table for carving will be needed. This carving table can be mounted on rollers so that it can be brought near the dining table when it is required. The sideboard may be of any fancied design that affords the convenience of shelves for plate and table ornaments, and drawers and undercloset for linen, cutlery, plate, and fine glassware. The drawers used for plates and the undercloset should be provided with locks.

China Closet. The china cabinet is a useful and beautiful article of furniture, but in the absence of such a cabinet any ordinary closet opening into the dining room may be utilized by replacing its door with a decorative door with diamond panes of glass or with a drapery hanging from a rod and drawn aside when the dining room is in use.

Sleeping Rooms

PROVIDE SEPARATE BEDS. Where two persons sleep in the same bed, the one who has the stronger physical power is likely to absorb the vital forces of the weaker one. Where either is afflicted with any tendency toward consumption, has any skin disease, or other malady, he is likely to impart its evil influences, if not its actual contagion, to the person who shares his bed with him.

SLEEP OUT OF DOORS IF POSSIBLE. Probably no practice would be more invigorating, healthful, or pleasurable than sleeping out of doors. In the vicinity of the great sanitariums, where sleeping out of doors has been proved to be a cure for consumption and other diseases, many persons have formed the habit of sleeping thus. Any porch somewhat excluded from view and in a sheltered location can be utilized. The porch should be screened and provided with storm curtains of tent canvas that can be drawn and buttoned like the curtains of a carriage.

Living out of doors

OUTFIT BEDROOMS WITH:

🌼 *Bed slips.* Bed linen often falls short of covering the mattress completely while in use; hence, the extra slip is needed, especially to protect from dust the underside of the mattress. These slips can be removed and laundered, twice a year or oftener, when housecleaning; pillow covers may be removed oftener if desired. Ticking treated in this way will be fresh and clean at the end of a dozen years' hard usage, when otherwise it would be so worn and soiled as to be unfit for use.

🌼 *Sheets.* Linen is, of course, the best material for comfort, appearance, and durability; but cotton sheeting is more commonly used because it is less expensive. Buy unbleached linen or cotton for sheets and pillow covers, as it is not only less expensive, but much more durable and can be easily bleached when being laundered.

🌺 *Feathers.* The best feathers for beds and pillows are plucked from live birds. Chicken, goose, or duck feathers may be preserved by putting the feathers together in a barrel after scalding. Leave the barrel open to the sun and rain, covering it with a screen to prevent the feathers from blowing about.

🌺 *Pillow-sham holder and lifter.* Few articles of household are as indispensable to ladies who pride themselves on having neat, tidy houses as the sham holder, a neat solution to the question of what to do with the shams at night. The holder consists of a light frame readily attached to any bedstead, upon which the shams are pinned or sewed to a tape and are held in their proper position during the day, either with or without a pillow under them. At night, by means of a spring, they are instantly raised up against the headboard of the bed.

☞

Upstairs are the bed-rooms, where the spotless linen and shining furniture invite repose. Such a house as this is not a very common thing to meet with amongst the settlers in the West, and it is easy to see that it is appreciated, when in the summer-time the stream of tourists begins to pour along the Pueblo road, from the number that seek for a night's lodging here and the earnestness with which they pray to be admitted.

—Brendan MacCarthy, "Home-Life in Colorado," in *Catholic World*, 1884

Advice to Housekeepers

Be orderly, but not fussy.

Look out for the easy way of doing things.

Set a good table but do not degenerate into a mere cook. Remember that "man does not live by bread alone."

"As much as lieth in you" come to the table with a cheerful face.

That husband's mother "always did it so" is no reason why you should adopt the plan.

A hearty laugh and a determination to see the "funny side" makes a very good sauce for a burnt pudding.

Have a way of your own. You may not be allowed to follow it in peace until you are fifty—but don't give up.

Never mind the complications in the "top bureau drawer."
Only you yourself can be affected by them, and they may prove a valuable safety-valve upon occasions.

Don't laugh when husband's collar button rolls under the bureau.

—How We Cook in Colorado, 1907

Miscellaneous Receipts for the Household

Remedies for Household Pests

  Cayenne pepper will keep the storeroom and pantry free from *ants* and *cockroaches*.

  Kerosene oil is a sure remedy for *red ants*. Place small blocks under a sugar barrel, so as not to let the oil touch the barrel.

- For *bugs* and *ants,* one may also dissolve 2 pounds alum in 3 quarts boiling water. Apply boiling hot with a brush. Add alum to whitewash for storerooms, pantries, and closets.
- Uncork a bottle of oil of pennyroyal, and it will drive away *mosquitoes* or other blood-sucking insects; they will not return so long as the scent of it is in the room.
- Mix a little powdered potash with meal and throw it into the rat holes and it will not fail to drive the *rats* away.

Fort Collins, September 10, 1873

My first experiences of Colorado travel have been rather severe. At Greeley I got a small upstairs room at first, but gave it up to a married couple with a child, and then had one downstairs no bigger than a cabin, with only a canvas partition. It was very hot, and every place was thick with black flies. The kitchen was the only sitting-room, so I shortly went to bed, to be awoke very soon by crawling creatures apparently in myriads. I struck a light, and found such swarms of bugs that I gathered myself up on the wooden chairs, and dozed uneasily till sunrise. Bugs are a great pest in Colorado. They come out of the earth, infest the wooden walls, and cannot be got rid of by any amount of cleanliness. Many careful housewives take their beds to pieces every week and put carbolic acid on them.

Isabella L. Bird, *A Lady's Life in the Rocky Mountains,* 1881

Death to the Bugs

This remedy is said to be infallible: Take two pounds of alum; bruise it, and reduce it nearly to powder; dissolve it in three quarts of boiling water, letting it remain in a warm place till the alum is dissolved. The alum water is to be applied hot, by means of a brush, to every joint and crevice. Brush the crevices in the floor of the skirting board if they are suspected places; white-wash the ceiling putting in alum, and there will be an end to their dropping from thence.

—*Darley Family Papers*, 186?

Cleaning and Polishing Furniture and Utensils

To CLEAN COPPER WARE. Wash and rub with half a lemon. Take a handful of common salt and enough vinegar and flour to make a paste, then mix together thoroughly. There is nothing better for cleaning coppers. After using the paste, wash thoroughly with hot water, rinse in cold water, and wipe dry.

To CLEAN ENAMELED WARE. Dampen a cloth, dip it in common soda, rub the ware briskly, wash and wipe dry. Or keep them clean by rubbing with sifted wood ashes or whitening. Care must be taken not to use lye in cleaning tins, as it will injure them

To CLEAN EARTHENWARE. Put in a kettle with cold water, ashes, and salt soda, bring to a boil, and after boiling let stand 24 hours in the lye; or fill the vessels with hot lime water and let them stand 24 hours.

To CLEAN GLASSWARE. Fill with buttermilk, let stand 48 hours, and wash in soapsuds. Or, put in 2 tablespoonsful of vinegar and 1 tablespoonful of baking soda. This will effervesce vigorously. Hold the article over the sink; if a decanter, do not cork or the vessel may burst.

To remove the yellow discoloration of china. Moisten a soft cloth in water and dip into dry salt, fine coal, or wood ashes and rub off the stain with it. Afterwards, wash with soap and water.

To clean draperies. Draperies and tapestries hung upon the walls may be cleaned by pouring gasoline into a shallow pan and brushing them with this by means of a soft brush or whisk broom.

To clean furniture. Mix ½ pint of linseed oil, ½ pint of vinegar, and ½ pint of turpentine. Apply with a flannel rag and rub with a dry flannel.

To polish furniture. Mix 1 pint of alcohol, 1 pint of spirits of turpentine, 1½ pints of raw linseed oil, 1 ounce balsam fir, and 1 ounce ether. Dilute the balsam with the alcohol, which will take about 12 hours. Mix the oil with the turpentine in a separate vessel and add the alcohol, and last the ether. Apply with a woolen cloth.

Gas was introduced several years ago, and the system, which now includes nearly all sections of the city, is being constantly improved and extended. The Brush electric light has been in very general use for nearly three years, and the Edison incandescent lamps are now being employed.

—E. Ingersoll, *The Crest of the Continent: A Summer's Ramble in the Rocky Mountains and Beyond,* 1885

CHAPTER NINE

---

*F*OR THE COOK APPOINTING HER KITCHEN

There are very few housekeepers indeed who could not—by intelligent forethought in planning and arranging the contents of the kitchen, pantry, and storeroom—save themselves daily miles of useless traveling to and fro.

Kitchen Furniture

STOVE. First, the housekeeper must have a good stove or range, and it is well for her to have the dealer at hand when it is put up, to see that it draws well. The woodwork near stoves and the collars above stovepipes, where they pass through the ceiling and walls, may be protected by a piece of hard, smooth asbestos board.

OVENS. Separate ovens should be used for meat and pastry because the particles of fat which fly from the meat while it is baking burn upon the sides of the oven and impart their odor and flavor to delicate cakes and pastry. The bread and pastry ovens do not require to be so hot as those in which meat is baked, and means must be devised to moderate their heat when it is excessive. All the flues and the top and bottom of the ovens should be kept free from ashes, and the dampers

should always be in good working order.

SINK. The sink may be of iron or other metal, stone, or even wood lined with lead, tin, or zinc. But it should stand on four legs. The sink should be placed high enough so that the dishes may be washed without stooping. A small shelf or cupboard above the sink to contain soap, borax, washing powder, and various utensils will be found convenient.

Air is admitted to every part

SINK-SIDE WORK TABLE. A bench or table, homemade if necessary, at the left of the kitchen sink and as large as the room will admit, is indispensable. Have the table overlap the edge of the sink and cover it with zinc, which will not rust. Turn up the zinc over a molding around the sides of the table, except at the end over the sink, so that water will drain back from it into the latter. Carry the zinc, if possible, 18 inches or 2 feet up the kitchen wall behind the table and the sink. This is lasting, easily kept clean, and is not injured by hot pans or kettles. If scrubbed clean it can be used as a molding board; particles of dough which adhere to it can easily be scraped off with a knife.

KITCHEN CABINET. A good kitchen cabinet with metal bins for flour, meal, and other substances that mice are fond of is an investment which will save time and strength for the housekeeper and will be a money-saver in the long run. These bins should be removable so that they can be regularly washed, scalded, and dried.

WORK TABLE. The kitchen table may be used as a work table if covered with oilcloth. This will last a long time if the table is padded with sheet wadding or several thicknesses of newspaper covered with an old sheet. Draw the padding smooth and tack it under the edge of the table.

TABLEWARE CABINET. Placing a china cabinet for the ordinary tableware just above the sink-side work table saves time and steps lost in walking from the sink to the table, and thence to pantry or closet.

STOOL. Provide a strong stool, high enough to allow sitting down at the sink to pare vegetables and for other purposes.

FOOTSTOOL. A footstool, convenient also as a receptacle for work, may be made of a common pine soap box; fasten the cover on the box with small hinges and put on the bottom four small castors. Line the box with plain white paper and cover. Excelsior, which can be got at any furniture store, is good to stuff the top and much cheaper than curled hair.

Caring for the Sink

Save your "drippings" until you have enough grease for a moderate size batch. Put into an iron pot, add some potash lye and boil. If the resultant "MIXTURE" does not look just right continue the boiling, and when you have satisfied yourself that you have made Soap, add enough boiling water to make very thin, stir well, and then pour into your sinks and closets. It is excellent for cleaning the sewers, but don't attempt it use it on your clothes or for any other purpose.

Follow these instructions carefully and you will always have the kindliest feelings towards the manufacturers,

**THE DUNWOODY BROS. SOAP CO.,
DENVER, COLORADO**

Other Useful Objects to Have About

For your own or your cook's convenience, provide your kitchen with:

WASHBOARD. Hang beside the sink a small washboard to rub out dishcloths and keep towels sweet and clean.

DISH DRAIN. Make a dish drain from an old dishpan by perforating the bottom with holes by means of a hammer and round wire nails. Place the draining pan to the left of the dishpan to avoid unnecessary handling. If the handles are front and back, as you face the dishpan, you will have fewer pieces of nicked china. If lye is used, and the dishwater is fairly hot and soapy, dishes rinsed with cold water will dry in the rack bright and shiny and not require wiping. Or, if thoroughly rinsed with hot water, they may be allowed to drain the same way.

The Priority of Good Order

Your husband may admire your grace and ease in society, your wit, your school day accomplishments of music and painting, but all in perfection will not atone for an ill-ordered kitchen, sour bread, muddy coffee, touched meats, un-palatable vegetables, indigestible pastry and the whole train of horrors that result from bad house-keeping.

—Custer County Women's Club

SLATE. A child's school slate hung on a nail, with a slate pencil attached by a strong cord, will be found a great convenience in ordering groceries. When any supplies run low, make a note on the slate of what is wanted; when the grocer calls, run over this list to refresh your mind. The slate is also useful for making a program each morning of the things to be done through the day. You will be surprised to find how quickly these things will be disposed of. When cooking or preparing company dinner, make a list of the articles to be prepared.

TOPPERS. Keep a nice flat-washed rock to weight down butter, beef, or tongues under brine; and stiff writing paper to dip in brandy and lay on top of preserves.

DINNER MATS. Dinner mats, either square or oval, made of two thicknesses of linen with an opening at one end to admit a square of asbestos, will prevent the hot tea or coffee pot or dishes containing hot food from injuring the tablecloth or the polished surface of the table.

STOVE MATS. Asbestos mats lined with wire have many uses about the stove. They may be placed in a hot oven to prevent cakes and pies from burning on the bottom and also on the top of the stove to prevent the contents of kettles and saucepans from burning. A small wire-lined asbestos mat, with a hole cut through the center but not through the wire, will be found useful for warming milk and other things in cups and small saucepans with rounded bottoms. The heat is applied to the bottom instead of the sides, and the vessel will not tip.

MATCH SAFE. Keep a stock of matches on a high, dry shelf in a covered earthen jar or tin box with a tight lid where they will be out of the way of children and safe from rats and mice. These animals are fond of phosphorus and will gnaw match heads if they can and often set them on fire. Have a covered match safe in each room where they are in frequent use; match safes fastened to sandpaper will be found a great convenience.

ASH RECEPTACLE. Keep a sheet-iron pan or scuttle to take up ashes.

SLEEVE PROTECTORS. An old pair of stockings may be converted into useful sleeve protectors by cutting off the feet and hemming the cut edge. These may be drawn over the sleeves of a clean gown if necessary when washing dishes.

DISHCLOTHS. Save and use cloth flour, sugar, salt, and cornmeal sacks, which keep white and last longer than ordinary towel stuff. You may also use scrim or cotton underwear crocheted about the edge or folded and hemmed double or the fiber of the so-called dishrag gourd, the seeds of which may be obtained from any seedman. Cheesecloth is good both for washing and wiping dishes, especially for drying silver and glassware.

STOCK THE KITCHEN WITH SUCH CONTAINERS AS:

- Milk vessels of tin or earthenware, never stoneware;
- Four buckets with close-fitting lids for setting aside milk for later—one for dinner, one for supper, one for breakfast, one for cooking purposes;
- Bottles and jugs to hold yeast while rising and walnut catsup while sunning;
- Stone jars to fill with brine in which to throw lemon peels to suit one's convenience and to store pickles, pack with shad, spices, and vinegar to set in boiling water for potted shad;
- Demijohn or runlet for storing wine;
- Glass jars for keeping preserves so they can be readily inspected;
- Firkin to hold rolls of butter and to keep boiled pigs feet closely covered to prevent them from molding before they are fried;
- Preserving kettle to put up corn in brine;
- Small, common glasses for keeping jellies;
- Wide-mouthed glass jars for keeping marmalade;
- Piggin for taking up butter.

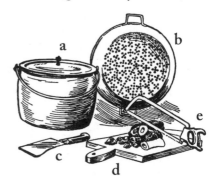

The Storeroom

Groceries and supplies for a household of any size should, if possible, be bought in quantity; therefore, every house should have a storeroom, appointed as follows.

MAKE A STOREROOM INEXPENSIVELY. A small storeroom can be made in a corner of the cellar at much less cost than is commonly supposed by putting up walls of concrete made of sand or gravel and cement. When furnished with a suitable door, this storeroom will be damp-proof and free from dust, germs, and all other unsanitary pests. There should be a cellar window protected on the outside by wire netting and having on the inside a removable screen of cheesecloth to keep out the dust. If you would have wholesome food, keep the window down at the top, night and day, except in the coldest weather.

INCLUDE AMPLE SHELVING. Slat shelves painted with white paint and a coat of enamel may be built up in the storeroom back to back, with just enough room between them for a person to walk, in the same manner as book stacks in a library. Preserves, pickles, canned goods, butter, eggs, and other groceries can be stored year-round in perfect safety.

HANG NETS FOR FRUIT. A suspended net or two should also be supplied for hanging lemons and oranges.

STOCK THE ROOM WITH EARTHENWARE. Earthenware jars are necessary for sugar, oatmeal, rice, tapioca, sago, barley, and spices. And, if it is wished to keep on hand the pound cake and fruit cake of our grandmothers (some cakes made from old-fashioned recipes given in this book will keep for years), no snugger quarters for their preservation can be found than earthen jars with tight-fitting lids inside the dry storeroom.

KEEP AN ACCOUNT BOOK. This is the room where you should enter the date when each item is bought and the price paid for it in your account book.

MAKE AN OUTDOOR CUPBOARD. Have you an outdoor cupboard in which to keep milk, meat, and fish during the cool weather of early spring and fall? A dry-goods box with a hinged locked door, nailed above the reach of cats and dogs against the arbor that covers the kitchen door, will save many a journey to the storeroom. It should have holes bored in the ends to allow a current to circulate through it, for food will keep fresher and sweeter in the open air.

Chapter Ten

$\mathcal{F}$or the Homemaker on the Grounds

In the Garden

I wish all my fair sisters would set apart a portion of their home grounds for the garden.

Consider the economic benefits. An area of land cultivated as a kitchen garden will easily supply the family table with $100 worth of vegetables every year.

Cultivate a flower garden for well-being. Best for the lady who tends the garden is that life-giving something in the very smell of the ground, especially in the soft springtime. And when long summer days come, when the lady drops her endless sewing and gathers what she has grown in anticipation of preparing a fresh meal, a vase of colorful blooms upon the table to meet the family when they sit will give her a lighter step and rosy cheeks. This is not romance but sound common sense.

Start small. Most women have their time quite fully occupied with the supervision of household matters. They would like to have some flowers, because a certain amount of work among them is refreshing, a resting spell because of its change from the monotony of work indoors. The cultivation of a small garden will not involve more labor than they can perform in odd spells, but if they attempt too much, the flowers will call for so much attention that the idea of rest and recreation is destroyed and they will fail to enjoy them. Begin cautiously and enlarge the operation as you feel justified in doing so.

But seems there is a legend, or an old philosophy,
That a spirit sometimes lingers in a blossom or a tree.
If it is not so, how is it that the human heart can see
Something there that wakes an answer like a thrill of sympathy?
Weeping willow, modest violet and the pansy think-of-me,
Laurel signalizes glory, and the broom humility;
But the ivy is for friendship, and it seemeth best of all,
'Tis the rose of love with petals that will never fade or fall.
And as friendship, saith the poet, is but 'love without his wings,'
Ivy is its chosen symbol for it closest, longest clings

—Will Housel, "Senior Class Day Poem, "
University of Colorado, 1889

PREPARE SOIL CAREFULLY. To prepare earth for seeds or small plants or for filling pots or window boxes, mix one part by bulk of well-rotted manure, two parts of good garden loam, and one part of sharp fine sand. Choose for this purpose manure which has been thoroughly rotted but not exposed to leaching from the weather. Mix all together in a heap, stir well with the shovel, sift, and place in bores or in the bed prepared for the seed. If convenient, bake the soil for an hour in a hot oven. This will kill all weed seed and spores of fungus disease.

☞ Water

The keeping of a turf and garden, after it is once begun, is merely a matter of watering. The garden is kept moist mainly by flooding from the irrigating ditch in the street or alley, but the turf of the lawn and the shrubbery owe their greenness to almost incessant sprinkling by the hand hose. Fountains are placed in nearly every yard.

—Ernest Ingersoll, *The Crest of the Continent: A Summer's Ramble in the Rocky Mountains and Beyond,* 1885

PROTECT PLANTS FROM THE WEATHER. To protect small plants from heat, drive stakes into the ground slanting toward the north and lean boards against them to shade the rows. Or use light frames on lath or wooden slate and cover them with cotton cloth. To protect crops planted in winter from cold and give an early start in spring, set the stakes slanting to the south and lean boards against them on the north side. Or cover with a mulch of manure, straw, or leaves. But take care that this is not so thick as to keep the air from the plants.

"Laying the Denver Dust" after Dinner

After dinner (for Denver dines at five o'clock as a rule), the father of the house lights his cigar and turns houseman for an hour while he chats with friends; or the small boys bribe each other to let them lay the dust in the street, to the imminent peril of passers-by; and young ladies escape the too engrossing attention of complimentary admirers by busily sprinkling heliotrope and mignonette, hinting at a possible different use of the weapon if admiration becomes too ardent. The swish and gurgle and sparkle of water are always present, and always must be; for so Denver defies the desert and dissipates the dreaded dust.

—Ernest Ingersoll, *The Crest of the Continent: A Summer's Ramble in the Rocky Mountains and Beyond,* 1885

CHOOSE OLD SEED DEALERS. If you send to the florist for seed—and it is always advisable to do that, for he makes a specialty of seed growing and knows how to produce the best—be sure to patronize a reliable dealer. There are always men in all kinds of business who are not to be trusted. The old seed farms are all reliable; their continuance in business proves that, for if they were not they would, after a little, lose customers and give up.

FORM A SEED CLUB. The packages of seeds put up by most seed growers generally contain more than one person will use. It is a good plan to club together in a country neighborhood. The cost will be less, and there will be seeds enough to divide among half a dozen persons.

On the first of September, 1881, E. T. Hotchkiss, myself and others came into the Valley of the North Fork and while making a stay of only one day, I discovered thorn apple and buffalo berry growing luxuriantly and in abundance. Therefore, with this evidence before me, I became strongly of the belief that many varieties of fruit might be grown here and resolved at once to make the trial.

—Samuel Wade,
Colorado Farmer, 1885

PLANT RASPBERRIES, BLACKBERRIES, CURRANTS, GOOSEBERRIES, AND GRAPES IN THE FALL. These fruits set out in fall, even in October, before the leaf drops, will make double the growth and double the fruit the next year than if planted in spring. I recommend early setting so that fall rains may settle the dirt nicely about the roots, and the fruits begin their growth with the opening of spring, even throwing out rootlets in the fall. Mulch before freezing with litter of any kind—manure, sawdust, sods, or straw—over each hill and they will come out all right in spring and begin to grow as soon as frost is out, scarcely a plant failing.

In the Barn and on the Farm

As the care and maintenance of domestic animals most frequently falls to the supervision of the farmwife, keep these brief thoughts in mind.

TREAT YOUR ANIMALS WITH KINDNESS. Curse and scream at them, and you excite their fears and injure their disposition to be kind. A pet today and a kick tomorrow will destroy their confidence in you and leads them to expect abuse rather than kindness.

BEWARE THE IMPATIENCE OF BOYS AND HIRED HELP. They are likely to think there is no way of showing their power over a horse but by jerking at the reins and yelling or cursing at him.

The cost of raising a three-year-old steer on any of the great cattle ranges of the west can safely be put down at $4.75. That is, at the present time. Of course, as time glides on and the humane feeling which now exists in the east shall invade the west, then the cost will be more, as the building of sheds, etc., for winter use will be necessary.

—Charles A. Siringo, *A Texas Cowboy of Fifteen Years on the Hurricane Deck of a Spanish Pony—Taken from Real Life*, 1886

DON'T KEEP THOSE YOU CAN'T FEED. One well-wintered horse is worth as much as two that drag through on straw. The same is true of oxen, and emphatically so of cows. The owner of a half-starved dog loses the use of him, for at the very time when he is most needed as a guard, he must be off scouring the country for food.

I killed a rattlesnake this morning close to the cabin, and have taken its rattle, which has eleven joints. My life is embittered by the abundance of these reptiles—rattlesnakes and moccasin snakes, both deadly, carpet snakes and "green racers," reputed dangerous, water snakes, tree snakes, and mouse snakes, harmless but abominable. Seven rattlesnakes have been killed just outside the cabin since I came. A snake, three feet long, was found coiled under the pillow of the sick woman. I see snakes in all withered twigs, and am ready to flee at "the sound of a shaken leaf." And besides snakes, the earth and air are alive and noisy with forms of insect life, large and small, stinging, humming, buzzing, striking, rasping, devouring!

—Isabella L. Bird, *A Lady's Life in the Rocky Mountains,* 1881

KEEP YOUR ANIMALS CLEAN. Cleanliness is indispensable if one would keep his animals healthy. In their original state all domestic animals are clean and healthy. The hog is not naturally a dirty animal. He enjoys currying as much as a horse or cow, and would be as careful of his litter as a cat if he had a fair chance.

REMEMBER, WHEN MILKING:

- Sit with the left knee close to the right hind leg of the cow and the head pressed against her flank.
- Put the fingers around the teat close to the bag. Firmly close the forefingers of each hand alternately, immediately

July 9, 1867

I went out to milk & one of the cows is afraid of me. I have milked her several times but tonight the wind blew very hard & she was afraid of my dress. It blew out just as I had commenced milking. She kicked me over & hurt my leg so I could hardly get to the house & tore a big hole in my dress and drawers.

—Amelia Butts (Mrs. George) Buss, *Diary,* 1866-1867

squeezing with the other fingers (the forefingers prevent the milk flowing back into the bag, while the others press it out).

- Keep the left hand always ready to ward off a blow from her feet, which the gentlest cow may give almost without knowing it, if her tender teats be cut by long nails or her bag be tender.
- Strip her dry every time she is milked, or she will dry up.
- If she gives much milk, it pays to milk three times a day.

Putting a minimum of indispensables into a bag, and slipping on my Hawaiian riding-dress over a silk skirt, and a dust-cloak over all, I stealthily crossed the *plaza* to the livery-stable, the largest building in Truckee, where twelve fine horses were stabled in stalls on each side of a broad drive. My friend of the evening before showed me his "rig," three velvet-covered side-saddles almost without horns. Some ladies, he said, used the horn of the Mexican saddle, but none "in this part" rode cavalier fashion. I felt abashed. I could not ride any distance in the conventional mode, and was just going to give up this splendid "ravage," when the man said, "Ride your own fashion; here, at Truckee, if anywhere in the world, people can do as they like." Blissful Truckee! In no time a large grey horse was "rigged out" in a handsome silver-bossed Mexican saddle, with ornamental leather tassels hanging from the stirrup-guards, and a housing of black bear's-skin. I strapped my silk skirt on the saddle, deposited my cloak in the corn-bin, and was safely on the horse's back before his owner had time to devise any way of mounting me. Neither he nor any of the loafers who had assembled showed the slightest sign of astonishment, but all were as respectful as possible.

—Isabella L. Bird, *A Lady's Life in the Rocky Mountains*, 1881

⚘ Do not feed fowls too much soft, wet feed; it is liable to affect their digestive organs. Grit, shell, dry bone, and charcoal, while perhaps not proper foods, are important accessories in raising fowls.

⚘ Oyster shells should be given to pullets when they show signs of laying, and should be always accessible to laying hens.

⚘ If you have not already received it, send for "Dr. Sloan's Advice" on the care and treatment of Horses, Cattle, Hogs, and Poultry. It tells how to cure Bramble-foot, Cholera, Diarrhea, Roup, and Worms with Sloan's Liniment and how to rid hens of lice.

—*Sloan's Cook Book and Advice to Housekeepers,* 1905

Miscellaneous Receipts for the Barn and Farm

TO FATTEN PIGS VERY FAT. Feed them on boiled rice.

TO GATHER AND PRESERVE ROOTS. Roots should be gathered in spring, with but few exceptions, and are better for being fresh. Roots to be dried should be well washed and sliced, unless they are preserved for the sake of the bark, when they must be merely washed and dried. The process of drying may be simply performed by stringing the pieces together, or scattering them on paper trays, and exposing them, for a sufficient time, to a gentle heat, say from 90 to 130 degrees Fahrenheit.

TO PROCURE ICE. Nearly fill a gallon stone bottle with hot spring water (leaving room for about a pint), and put in two ounces of refined nitre; the bottle must then be stopped very close and let down into a deep well. After three or four hours it will be completely frozen, but the bottle must be broken to procure the ice. If the bottle is moved up and down, so as to be sometimes in and sometimes out of the water, the consequent evaporation will hasten the process.

COMPOSITION TO HEAL WOUNDS IN TREES. Mix four parts chalk, two parts tar, and one part brick dust. Melt and apply warm.

TO DRIVE BUGS FROM VINES. The ravage of the yellow-striped bug on cucumbers and melons may be prevented by sifting charcoal dust over the plants; if repeated three or four times, the plants will be entirely freed from annoyance. There is in charcoal some property so noxious to these troublesome insects, that they fly from it the instant it is applied.

TO NOURISH A FARM HORSE AT WORK. A small horse that is driven or worked should have 2 quarts at a feed, given 3 times a day, with 5 pounds of hay (cut), night and morning. And a horse that is not working, but will be soon, would be the better for a daily feed of 2 quarts of grain (oats) given at noon. An excellent mixture of grain is cracked 1 bushel corn and 2 bushels oats.

TO SAVE OATS IN FEEDING HORSES. Bruise or crush your oats in a mill, and your horse will become fatter on half his usual allowance of these oats than he was before on double the quantity unprepared. If you cannot bruise the oats, pour hot water on them and let them soak for a few hours.

To CURE THE RED WATER IN CATTLE. Take 1 ounce Armenian bole, a ½ ounce dragon's blood, 2 ounces Castile soap, and 1 dram rock-alum. Dissolve these in a quart of hot ale or beer, and let it stand until it is blood-warm. Give this as one dose, and, if it should have the desired effect, give the same quantity about 12 hours after. This is an excellent medicine for changing the water and acts as a purgative.

WARTS ON COWS' TEATS OR THE HAND'S REMEDY. Take a handful of green bean leaves and rub them in the hands until the hands are thoroughly wet with the juice; then proceed to milk. As often as the hands get dry while milking, moisten again with the bean leaf juice. Do this twice or three times a week, and in a few weeks there will be no warts on the cow's teats or the hands of the milker.

SIMPLE BUT CERTAIN REMEDY FOR EGG-EATING HENS. Make an opening in the large end of an egg and let out the contents, beat them up, mix into them enough strong mustard to refill the egg, and paste on a bit of cloth to keep the contents in. Then place the egg where the egg-eaters can see and get at it. They will "go for it" at once and as quickly go away. It is too much for them. And as they take it for granted that all eggs are alike, they give up the habit. I cannot see why it would not be as good for egg-eating dogs as for hens.

The most absorbing part of the "Woman's question" of the present time is the remedy for the varied sufferings of women who are widows or unmarried, and without means of support. ... A woman can invest capital in the dairy and qualify herself to superintend a dairy farm as well as a man. ... And, too, the raising of poultry, of hogs, and of sheep are all within the reach of a woman with proper abilities and training for this business. So that, if a woman chooses, she can find employment both interesting and profitable in studying the care of domestic animals.

—*Miss Beecher's Housekeeper and Healthkeeper,* 1873

CHAPTER ELEVEN

$\mathcal{F}$OR THE COOK AT HER TASKS

The turnpike road to people's hearts, I find,
Lies through their mouths, or I mistake mankind.

—*The Mesa Workers' Cook Book, 1897*

Preparing Common Foods

Herein lie bits of wisdom earned with experience regarding the general preparation of the foods we most often consume. These are matters often taken for granted by cooks of some years and left out of so many recipes.

Bread

"When the bread rises in the oven, the heart of the housewife rises with it." The speaker of this truth might have added that the heart of the house-wife sinks in sympathy with the sinking bread.

USE GOOD FLOUR. Good flour is an indispensable requisite to good bread and, next, good yeast and sufficient kneading. Only experience will enable you to be a good judge of flour. One test is to rub the dry flour between your fingers; if the grains feel round, it is a sign that the flour is good. If after trying a barrel of flour twice, you find it becomes wet and sticky, after being made up of the proper consistency, you had better then return it to your grocer.

To Make Home Happy

The most important of all things pertaining to the Kitchen and Cookery, to happiness and Health, is the "Staff of Life," otherwise GOOD BREAD and BISCUITS, to say nothing of the thousand and one delicacies of Cakes, Waffles, Puddings, Pies, etc., that the children love so much, and which, when well made and properly cooked, are no detriment to health, but are, on the contrary, both nourishing and of the greatest value in giving variety to the somewhat monotonous routine of Meat and Vegetables that go to make up the Bill of Fare of the average American family.

—*Cow Brand Soda Cook Book and Facts Worth Knowing*, 1900

SUN AND AIR FLOUR BEFORE USE. In the morning, get out the flour to be made up at night for next morning's breakfast. Sift it in a tray and put it out in the sun, or, if the day is damp, set it near the kitchen fire.

SET BREAD TO RISE BY SEASON. Set bread to rise in a cool place in summer but in a warm place, free from draughts, in winter. In the latter season, the crock may be wrapped in a blanket or set on bread-warming shelf under which a lighted coal-oil lamp is placed.

HANDLE DOUGH LIGHTLY. Never knead bread a second time after it rises, as this ruins it. Handle as lightly as possible, make into the desired shapes, and put into the molds in which it is to be baked. Use a little lard on the hands when making out the loaf, or else dip a feather in lard and pass lightly over the bread just before putting it in the oven to bake, so as to keep the crust from being too hard. The top

☞ To Make Good Yeast

Take 5 or 6 good-sized potatoes, then pour 2 quarts of boiling water to them, also drop in a small handful of hops tied in a bag. Take potatoes out when done and mash them, take out hops, then make 1 ½ teacups of flour in a smooth paste and stir in the hop tea; let boil 5 minutes. Then put in the mashed potatoes, take off the fire, and put in a ½ cup of good yeast or leaven. Keep in a warm place till it rises well, then tie up close and put away till needed, or make leaven.

—*The Capitol Cook Book,* 1899

must be pricked or cut across so that the crust will not bind. Let it be a little warmer during the second rise than during the first. Always shape and put in the molds two hours before breakfast.

LEARN OVEN PLACEMENT. Set bread on the floor of the stove, never on the shelf, since the air is hot at the top of the oven. If you bake your dough hard on top first, it would not rise. We wish to have the yeast swell the starch and send the water that is in the dough in steam out through the holes we pricked in the loaf. As you set the bread in the stove, lay a piece of stiff writing paper over it to keep it from browning before heating through. Leave the door ajar a few minutes, then remove the paper and shut the door. When the top of the loaf is a light amber color, put back the paper so the bread may not brown too much while thoroughly baking. Turn the mold around so that each part may be exposed to equal heat. Have an empty baking pan on the shelf above the bread to prevent it from blistering.

INTRODUCE VARIETY. Do not constantly make bread in the same shapes; each morning, try to have some variation. Plain light bread dough may be made into loaves, rolls, twists, turn-overs, and light biscuits; these changes of shape make a pleasant and appetizing variety in the appearance of the table. Very pretty iron shapes (eight or twelve in a group, joined together) may be procured from almost any tinner.

☞ *Cooking in High Altitudes*

It is a well-established fact that in a high altitude the science culinary has its local and peculiar laws. It is commonly held that a different proportion of ingredients is necessary, as well as a different length of time. It is even claimed by some that more fuel is required here than in a lower altitude. Be this as it may, it is well established that the husband, who has recently brought his wife from the East, is not in healthy employment when he reminds her of the superior quality of his mother's cooking. He must wait until she has learned the new conditions in her new world.

—*Cloud City Cook-Book,* 1889

Tea and Coffee

BOIL DIFFERENT TEA TYPES FOR DIFFERENT TIMES. Of all "cups that cheer," there is nothing like the smoking hot cup of tea, made with boiling water, in a thoroughly scalded teapot. And if it is the good old-fashioned green tea of "ye ancient time," you must just put it to draw and not to boil; if it is genuine "English Breakfast" or best black tea, the water must not only be boiling hot at the very moment of pouring it on, but the tea must actually boil for at least five or ten minutes.

MAKE A TEAPOT BONNET. To insure keeping hot while serving, make the simple contrivance known as a "bonnet," which is warranted a sure preventive against that most insipid of all drinks—a warmish cup of tea. It is a sack with a loose elastic in the bottom, large enough to cover the entire teapot. Draw this over the teapot as soon as the tea is poured into it.

More common sense is required in bread making than in any other branch of cooking. On account of different grades of soda, cream of tartar, baking powder, and yeast, it is impossible to be accurate as to the exact amount to use.

Where sour milk is used, a young cook had just as well make up her mind to taste uncooked bread, so as to ascertain whether there is not enough or too much soda, as this is the only way to succeed every time.

—The Capitol Cook Book, 1899

Milk and Butter

The most exquisite nicety and care must be observed in the management of milk and butter.

KEEP ON HAND TWO SETS OF VESSELS. A housekeeper should have two sets of milk vessels (tin or earthenware, never stoneware, as this is an absorbent). She should never use twice in succession the same milk vessels without having them scalded and aired.

SET ASIDE PLENTY. In warm weather, sweet milk should be set on ice or in a spring house. Never put ice in sweet milk; this dilutes it. One pan of milk should be set aside to raise cream for coffee. One bucket with a close-fitting lid should be filled with milk and set aside for dinner, one for supper, one for breakfast, and a fourth for cooking purposes.

CHURN CAREFULLY. To make butter, strain unskimmed milk into a scalded churn, where the churning is done daily. This will give a sweeter butter and nicer buttermilk than when cream is skimmed and kept for churning. Do not let the

☞ To Make Butter

Scald the churn thoroughly, then cool well with spring water. Next pour in the thick cream. Churn fast at first, then, as the butter forms, more slowly; always with perfect regularity. In warm weather, pour a little cold water into the churn, should the butter form slowly. In the winter, use warm water for the same purpose. When the butter has "come" rinse the blades of the churn with cold water and take up the butter with a wooden ladle. When you have collected all the butter, drain off excess water, squeezing and pressing the butter with a ladle until all milk is removed. Add a little salt, then mold or put in pats.

☞ Brine That Preserves Butter a Year

To 3 gallons of brine strong enough to bear an egg, add ¼ pound good loaf sugar and 1 tablespoonful of saltpeter, boil the brine and when it is cold, strain carefully. Pack butter in small jars and allow the brine to cover the butter to a depth of at least 4 inches. This completely excludes the air. If practical make your butter into small rolls, wrap each carefully in a clean muslin cloth, tying up with a string. Place a weight over the butter to keep it all submerged in the brine.

—Custer County Women's Club

milk in the churn exceed blood heat. If overheated, butter will be white and frothy and milk thin and sour. Churn as soon as the milk is turned. In summer, churn early in the morning, as fewer flies are swarming then, and the butter can be made much firmer.

PRINT AND REFRIGERATE CORRECTLY. Butter should be printed early in the morning, while it is cool. A plateful for each of the three meals should be placed in the refrigerator. Do not set butter in a refrigerator or a safe with anything else in it but milk. It readily imbibes the flavor of everything near it.

Eggs

While eggs are nourishing, they are not so heating to the blood as meat, and doctors often order them for patients who need nourishment yet cannot have their blood heated by meat juices. Even when they cost the most, you can really get more nourishment from them than for the same amount of money spent for meat.

TRY SHIRRING EGGS. This is a modification of baking eggs. Butter small earthen dishes and put an egg into each one without mixing the white and yolk; dust a little salt and pepper over the eggs. The eggs should be covered with buttered paper to prevent browning on the surface. The dishes are then placed upon the back of the stove or in a moderate oven. When the whites of the eggs are set, the dishes are then sent to the table.

TRY VARIOUS OMELETS. There is an infinite variety of omelets named from the special flavor or seasoning given by any predominating ingredient. The sweet light omelets are used for breakfast or plain desserts; the plain omelets are suitable for breakfast and luncheon. In parsley and fine herb omelets, the chopped herbs are mixed with the eggs before the omelet is cooked; grated ham, tongue, and cheese are also mixed in the same way. In other omelets, the special ingredient used is enclosed in the omelet.

DYE EGGS FOR EASTER. Easter morning would be incomplete, for the children at least, without the brightly colored eggs. When prepared dye stuffs are not available, varied colors may be produced by boiling a small quantity of the following with the eggs: for red, Brazil wood; for yellow, Persian berries or a little turmeric; for brown, a strong dye of turmeric; for a claret color, logwood; for black, logwood and chromate of potash; for blue, a mixture of powdered indigo and crystals of sulphate or iron; for reddish purple, red onion skins.

Common Meats and Game

HEED THESE KEEPING TIMES BEFORE USING PREPARED MEATS:

⤚ Soak all hams 24 hours before cooking.

⤚ Corn beef must remain packed down in salt for 10 or 12 days before being put in brine. It is fit for use after two weeks under the brine.

⤚ Spiced beef must remain three to four weeks in a wooden box or tub, in which it is turned occasionally in the pickle it makes and rubbed with salt.

⤚ Before hanging beef to smoke, it must remain for ten days in the salt, brown sugar, molasses, and saltpeter that has been rubbed on it.

⤚ Allow three weeks to prepare cured beef ham for use; let it remain in molasses a day and two nights and in molasses and salt for ten additional days; hang it up to dry for one week, then smoke it a little and keep hanging till used.

⤚ When the weather will admit of it, mutton is better for being kept a few days before cooking.

⤚ Truffle dressing is usually placed in the turkey two days beforehand to impart its flavor to the fowl.

☛ *Meat Relishes and Sauces*

Serve mint sauce with roast lamb.

Serve apple sauce with roast pork.

Serve horseradish with boiled beef.

Serve currant jelly with roast turkey.

Serve grape jelly with roast goose.

—*How We Cook in Colorado*, 1907

⤚ A goose must never be eaten the same day it is killed; if the weather is cold, it should be kept a week before using and before cooking should lie several hours in weak saltwater to remove the strong taste.

⤚ Kill young ducks some days before using; or, if obliged to use them the same day as killed, they are better roasted.

ROAST MEAT BEFORE AN OPEN FIRE. Use salt, pepper, butter, or lard, and dredge the meat with flour before roasting, but use little salt at first, as it hardens meat. Baste meat frequently to prevent it from hardening on the outside and to preserve the juices. If possible, roast the meat on a spit before a large, open fire, where there is the intense heat required for cooking and the constantly changing current of air necessary to carry away from the meat the fumes of burning fat, which impair its flavor.

The faults in the meat generally furnished to us are, first, that it is too new. A beefsteak, which three or four days of keeping might render practicable, is served up to us palpitating with freshness, with all the toughness of animal muscle yet warm.

—Harriet Beecher Stowe, *House and Home Papers,* 1869

KEEP MEAT FLAVORING ON HAND. As the housekeeper is sometimes hurried in preparing a dish, it will save time and trouble for her to keep on hand a bottle of meat flavoring compounded by putting in a quart bottle and covering with cider vinegar: 2 chopped onions, 3 pods of red pepper (chopped), 2 tablespoonsful brown sugar, 1 tablespoonful each of celery seed and ground mustard, and 1 teaspoonful each of black pepper and salt. A tablespoonful of this mixed in a stew, steak, or gravy will impart not only a fine flavor but a rich color.

Calf

ASK THE BUTCHER TO PREPARE IT SOMEWHAT. Have the butcher to remove the hair by scalding and scraping, to remove the teeth and the eyes from the head, and to split the head in two pieces without cutting the tongue or brains. Likewise, have him split the feet.

PREPARE THE BRAIN FOR SERVING. The brain may be heated in any good sauce and served as a separate dish. It may also be made into fritters or croquettes or into force-meat balls for garnishing the calf's

The introduction of cooking-stoves offers to careless domestics facilities for gradually drying-up meats, and despoiling them of all flavor and nutriment, facilities which appear to be very generally laid hold of. They have almost banished the genuine, old-fashioned roast-meat from our tables, and left in its stead dried meats with their most precious and nutritive juices evaporated. How few cooks, unassisted, are competent to the simple process of broiling a beefsteak or mutton chop! How very generally one has to choose between these meats gradually dried away, or burned on the outside and raw within!

—Harriet Beecher Stowe,
House and Home Papers, 1869

head by mixing it with an equal quantity of breadcrumbs, two raw eggs, and salt and pepper, and then either frying or poaching.

PREPARE THE TRIPE FOR SERVING. It should be boiled until tender in salted water and then scraped with the back of a knife; after that it can be pickled in scalding-hot spiced vinegar or kept in milk or buttermilk for several days. In the country, it may be necessary to prepare tripe for cooking by cleaning it with either lime water or with lye made from wood ashes. Tripe is usually broiled or fried, sometimes being first breaded or rolled in flour. It is an excellent winter food when some of the meats are scarce and expensive. If prepared for the table after the first boiling it requires high seasoning.

Pork

SELECT YOUNG PIGS FOR ROASTING. A roasting pig is in prime condition when it is three to six weeks old, with a soft, clean, pinkish white skin, plump hams, a short curly tail, thin delicate ears, and a soft, fringe-like margin all around the tongue.

PREPARE THE PIG FOR ROASTING. As soon as it is killed, plunge it into cold water for five minutes; then rub it all over with powdered resin and put it into scalding water for one minute. Lay it on a clean board and pull and scrape off the bristles, taking care not to injure the skin. When all the bristles are removed, wash the pig thoroughly, first in warm water and then several times in plenty of cold water. Then slit the pig from the throat downward and take out the entrails, laying the heart, liver, lights, and spleen in cold salted water. Wash the pig again in cold water, and wrap it from the air with a cloth wet in cold water until it is wanted for use.

BUTCHER THE HOG PROPERLY:

❀ After being properly dressed, hogs should hang long enough to get rid of the animal heat.

❀ When they are ready to be cut up, they should be divided into nine principal parts: two hams, two shoulders, two middlings, the head or face, the jowl, and the chine.

❀ The hog is laid on its back to be cut up.

❀ The head is cut off just below the ears, then it is split down each side of the backbone, which is the chine.

❀ This is divided into three pieces, the upper portion being a choice piece to be eaten cold.

❀ This fat portion may be cut off to make lard.

❀ Each half should then have the loaf fat taken out by cutting the thin skin between it and the ribs.

❀ Just under this, the next thing to be removed is the mousepiece or tenderloin, commencing at the point of the ham. This is considered the most delicate part and is used to make the nicest sausage.

❀ Just under this tenderloin are some short ribs about three inches long, running up from the point of the ham. This portion is removed by a sharp knife being run under it, taking care to cut it smooth and not too thick. When broiled, it is as nice as a partridge.

❀ The ribs are next taken out of the shoulder and middling,

though some persons prefer leaving them in the middling; in this case, seven should be taken from the shoulder to make a delicious broil.

※ Then cut off the ham as near the bone as possible, in a half circle. The shoulder is then cut square across.

※ The feet are then chopped off with a sharp cleaver. From the shoulder, they should be cut off leaving a stump of about two inches; from the ham, they should be cut off at the joint as smoothly as possible.

SALT THE HAMS. In order to impart redness to the hams, rub on each a teaspoon of pulverized saltpeter before salting. If the weather is very cold, warm the salt before applying it. First, rub and salt the skin side well, and then the fleshy side, using for the purpose a shoe sole or leather glove. No more salt should be used than a sufficiency to preserve the meat, as an excess hardens the meat. A bushel of salt is sufficient for a thousand pounds of meat. For the chine and ribs, a very light sprinkling of salt will suffice.

Game

STUFF AND ROAST. For partridges, pheasants, quails, or grouse, carefully cut out all the shot, wash thoroughly but quickly, using soda in the water; rinse again and dry with a clean cloth. Stuff them and sew them up. Skewer the legs and wings to the body, larder the breast with very thin slices of fat salt pork, place them in the oven, and baste with butter and water before taking up, having seasoned them with salt and pepper. Or you can leave out the pork and use only butter or cook them without stuffing. Make a gravy of the drippings, thickened with browned flour. Boil up and serve in a boat.

Small Birds Barded

BROIL AND SERVE WITH GRAVY. These are all very fine broiled, first splitting down the back, placing on the gridiron the inside down, cover with a baking tin, and broil slowly at first. Serve with cream gravy.

Terrapin

Terrapin is distinctive enough to be made a separate course at dinner. Only the flesh, eggs, and liver of terrapin are ordinarily used. Madeira is the proper wine to serve with terrapin.

Dress it properly:

❧ Loosen the sides of the shells of boiled terrapin, as soon as they are cool enough to handle.

❧ Lift off the top shell; pull or cut apart the small bands of flesh which hold it to the spine of the terrapin; then rein the under-shell. The entrails of the terrapin have the eggs and liver embedded in them, and the legs are attached to them by crossing bands of flesh.

❧ Pull off the legs, leaving the flesh attached to them; break off the sharp claws at the extremities of the feet; separate and throw away the head; and put the legs on a dish.

❧ Carefully remove the eggs and put them into a bowl of hot water.

❧ Separate the liver from the entrails and cut out that part of the liver which contains the small dark-green gall-bag that can be seen at one side of the liver. The utmost care should taken to avoid cutting or breaking the gall-bag; in removing it, the liver should be held over an empty dish, and if the gall-bag is cut or broken, the liver should be thrown away and the hands washed before the dressing of the terrapin is resumed.

❧ Cut the liver into half-inch squares and put it with the flesh of the terrapin.

Fish

Fish is a healthful and digestible food. Though not nearly so nutritious as meat, it is considered by many physicians a good brain food, especially if it is broiled.

Flour	$23.00 a hundred lbs.
Meal	$20.00 a hundred lbs.
Bacon	$30.00 a hundred lbs.
Ham	$45.00 a hundred lbs.
Shoulders	$30.00–35.00 a hundred lbs.
Mackerel	$35.00 a keg or $0.40 a lb.
Lard	$0.55 a lb., bucket $0.50 extra
Butter: States	$0.75 a lb., bucket $0.50 extra
Colo. Ranch	$1.30 a lb., bucket $0.50 extra
Eggs: Rance	$2.00–2.50 a doz.
Cheese: Hamburg	$0.50–0.60 a lb.
Tea	$2.50 – 3.00 a lb.
Coffee: Java	$0.75 a lb.
Rio	$0.55–0.60 a lb.
Brown Sugar	$0.40 a lb.
Powdered Sugar	$0.45 a lb.
Golden Syrup	$40.00 a keg, $4.50 a gallon
Dried apples	$0.40 a lb.
Dried peaches	$0.50 a lb.
Dried raspberries	$1.10 a lb.
Dried Blackberries	$0.80 a lb.
Canned Fruits/Vege.	$0.90–1.10 a can
Spuds	$0.20–0.25 a lb.
Turnip	$0.10 a lb.
Crackers	$0.35–0.40 a lb.
Candy	$1.00 a lb.

—August Hauck Block Collection

Caper Sauce for Boiled Mutton

2 ounces of butter; 1 dessertspoonful of flour; salt to taste; ½ pint of water; 3 dessertspoonsful of capers; 1 dessertspoonful of thin liquor; mix the flour and water to smooth paste; put into a saucepan and add the butter, and let boil 2 minutes; then add other ingredients. Nasturtium seeds can be used in place of capers.

—I. B., Denver, *The Twenty-Third Avenue Presbyterian Cook Book,* 1897

Wine Sauce for Game

½ glass of currant jelly, ½ glass of port wine, ½ glass of water, 1 tablespoonful of cold butter, 1 teaspoonful of salt, the juice of ½ lemon, 1 pinch of cayenne pepper, 3 cloves. Simmer all together a few minutes, adding the wine after it is strained. A few spoonsful of the gravy from the game may be added to it. This sauce is especially nice with venison.

—Tabor House, Denver, *The White House Cook Book,* 1887

Gooseberry Catsup

To 10 pounds or 8 quarts green berries, well cleaned and stemmed, add 7 pounds brown sugar, 2 teaspoonsful cinnamon, 1 teaspoonful allspice, 1 teaspoonful cloves, 1 pint cider vinegar. If not sweet enough, add 2 or 3 cupsful granulated sugar. Cook hard, stirring constantly, 3 or 4 hours.

—Elizabeth Van Keuren, Pueblo, *The Mesa Workers' Cook Book,* 1897

PRESERVE LIVING FISH. Stop their mouths up with crumbs of bread steeped in brandy, pour a very small quantity of brandy into them, and pack them in clean straw. In this way, it is said fish may be preserved in a torpid state for 12 or 15 days, and when put into water will come to life again after three or four hours.

CLEAN AGAIN AT HOME. Although fish should be cleaned at the market, one should not trust entirely to such cleaning, but pass the edge of the knife over the fish to remove any remaining scales. Wash it inside and out with a wet cloth, and dry carefully with a towel. Rub it next with salt and pepper and lay it on a dish or hang it up till you are ready to cook. Never keep it lying in water, either in preparing it for cooking or in trying to keep it till the next day.

COOK FISH ONE OF THESE FOUR WAYS:

Before boiling, rub fish carefully with a little vinegar. Boil in salted boiling water, with one tablespoonful vinegar, allowing ten minutes to a pound. Try with a needle; if it runs through easily, the fish is done. It will require an hour to boil a large fish and about 20 minutes for a small one.

Be careful to have boiling hot lard in the frying pan when you go to fry fish. First rub salt and pepper and flour or meal on the fish, then keep it covered while frying until it reaches a pretty amber color.

Fish which are either watery or very oily are best when cooked with direct exposure to the fire. Before broiling, rub with pepper and salt and then grease with fresh butter. Lay the fish on a gridiron well greased with sweet lard and lay the tin sheet over it. When you wish to turn, take the gridiron from the fire, holding the tin sheet on top of the fish; hold them together, lay them on a table with the tin sheet down and the gridiron uppermost, raise the gridiron, and easily slide the fish onto it to put it again on the fire and brown the other side, putting the tin sheet back on top of it. When done, lay the fish on a dish and pour sauce over it.

Sauce Hollandaise for Baked Fish

3 yolks of eggs, 2 teaspoonsful flour, 1 gill water; season with pepper, salt, mustard, and lemon juice. When partially cool, add 3 ounces melted butter.

—Mrs. M. J. Galligan, Pueblo,
The Mesa Workers' Cook Book, 1897

Gash fish for baking straight across—a half-inch deep, two inches long, and one inch apart—and lay in strips of pork. Place in pan and cover the bottom with water a half-inch deep; add one teaspoon of butter and one tablespoonful of salt. Dredge fish with flour and baste often. Keep up your supply of gravy as it boils away. Try with a knitting needle and take up with a cake turner.

To lard fish for baking, remove a large piece of the skin from the back of the fish and insert the lardoon. The lardoons are protected by buttered paper until the fish is nearly done; then the paper is removed to permit them to brown.

PREPARE SAUCES FOR SOME FISH. The very dry-fleshed fish should be served with a sauce. Whitefish have far less oil distributed through their bodies and are therefore not so rich as darker-colored fish, and need richer sauces and dressings. In making sauces for fish, never use the water in which the fish has been boiled. Larded fish is generally stuffed and served with a brown mushroom sauce.

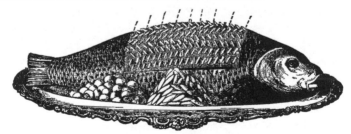

Fish larded and baked

Vegetables

During the summer, if you can get them fresh and cook them nicely, you will not need to buy nearly as much meat and can make many nice dishes, mostly all vegetables.

BOIL OR DRY CORN. Cold-boiled corn, cut from the ear and mixed with an equal quantity of cold potatoes chopped, can be fried with salt, pepper, and butter or heated with cold stewed tomatoes and served on toast. Or, cut the grains from ears of tender corn, spread them on large sheets of paper in the sun, and dry them thoroughly; or put them on pans in a cool oven and dry them. After the corn is dried, keep it in a cool, dry place. When it is wanted for the table, soak it overnight in enough water or milk to cover it; the next day boil it tender in the same water, season it with salt, pepper, and butter, and serve it hot.

DON'T ADD COLD MILK FOR MASHING POTATOES. Mashed potatoes will be hard, sticky, and heavy if you turn cold milk upon them while they are steaming hot; by adding scalding milk and beating them thoroughly, they will be light and feathery. Until served, they should be covered close with a napkin.

USE SCALDING OIL FOR FRYING POTATOES. Fried potatoes will be soaked and leathery if the fat is not hot enough and if they are not well drained when taken out.

PROCURE PLENTY OF SPINACH. In respect to quantity, spinach is desperately deceitful. I never see it drained after it is boiled without thinking of a young housekeeper who purchased a quart of spinach and ordered a spring dinner for herself and husband. When it should have appeared upon the table, there came in its stead a platter of sliced egg, she having given out one for the dressing. "Where is the spinach?" she demanded of the maid. "Under the egg, ma'am!" And it was really all there. The moral: Get enough spinach to be visible to the naked eye. A peck is not too much for a family of four or five.

Relishes

The innumerable small appetizers known as relishes, or hors d'oeuvres, include all forms of pickles and table sauces, small sandwiches and crusts garnished with highly seasoned meats, various preparations of cheese and eggs; in short, any small, highly spiced or seasoned dish calculated to rouse or stimulate the appetite.

CONSIDER THESE RELISHES:

☛ *Smoked Fish.* Small strips of cured fish, either salted or smoked, are acceptable as a relish; or small fish which have been preserved in oil, such as anchovies or sardines, may be wiped dry with a towel and served with vinegar or lemon juice. Smoked eels, herring, halibut, sturgeon, tunny-fish, salt cod, salmon, Finnan haddie, Yarmouth bloaters, or any dried fish may be served; only it must be delicately prepared in small pieces and with some suitable garnish, so as to be an appreciable incentive to the enjoyment of the heavier dishes which succeed it. Sliced lemon is always a good garnish for any highly seasoned relish.

☛ *Sandwich Butter.* Mix together equal parts good butter and grated ham or tongue; season rather highly with salt, cayenne, and mustard mixed with vinegar. Pack the mixture into little earthen jars; cover each jar with a piece of paper dipped in brandy and then exclude the air by a tight cover or a bladder wet and then tied over the top; keep in a cool, dry place. The flavor may be changed by varying the ingredients and seasoning.

Relishes

☛ *Canapés.* Canapés are small slices of bread slightly hollowed out on the upper surface and then fried golden brown in plenty of smoking hot fat. The little hollow is filled with any highly seasoned meat and the canapés served either hot or cold.

CONSIDER PICKLES AS REL-
ISHES AND HEED THESE
PICKLING TIMES:

❀ Oysters must stand two days covered in stewed juice and vinegar to become pickled.

❀ Three weeks is long enough for green pickles to remain in brine, if you wish to make your pickle early in the fall.

❀ Yellow pickle must stand for two 24-hour periods in brine, poured over while hot; on the third day, spread them on a board or table and let them stand in the hot sun four days, taking care that no dew shall fall on them.

❀ For boiled cucumber pickle, take fresh cucumbers, put them in brine for a few days, then take them out and put them in vinegar to soak for two days.

☛ Cucumber Mangoes (Prize Recipe)

Soak in strong brine 9 days as many large green cucumbers as you wish to use. Then lay them 48 hours in clear water. Cut a slit lengthwise in each, scoop out seeds, wipe dry, and fill with stoned raisins, lemon cut in long, thin strips, and 6 or 8 whole cloves. Sew up slit, pack cucumbers in a stone jar, and cover with a boiling sirup made after following recipe: Add to 1 quart vinegar 5 pounds sugar, also mace, cinnamon, and cloves to taste. Reheat sirup and pour boiling hot over cucumbers for 9 successive mornings.

—Mrs. John F. Shafroth, Wife of Governor of Colorado, *Mrs. Curtis's Cook Book: A Manual of Instruction in the Art of Everyday Cookery*, 1909

❀ Sweet tomato pickle will be ready for use in a fortnight after being prepared, poured into a stone jar, and sealed tight.

❀ Walnuts to be pickled remain in saltwater five or six weeks, then in fresh water for 24 hours, and are ready for use in two or three weeks.

❀ Keep martinas covered in very strong brine for ten days, then wash and put them in vinegar to stand ten more days before putting them in the jar intended for them.

☒ To stop fruit pies from running over, bind them with a damp white cloth two inches wide. Let it extend over the edge of the pie into the pan.

—*The Mesa Workers' Cook Book,* 1897

☒ If you wish your pies to brown nicely, sprinkle a little sugar in the bottom of your oven.

—*Western Slope Cook Book,* 1912

☒ To make pie meringue crisp instead of tough, add a pinch of cornstarch to meringue.

—*Western Slope Cook Book,* 1912

Desserts

SELECT DESSERTS BY THE DINNER. When you have a hearty, salt-meat dinner, use a cold, light, delicate pudding, like a boiled custard. When you have a fish dinner, which does not give the nourishment that meat does, serve a boiled, hearty pudding. A lemon cornstarch pudding can be used when you are short of milk, and a broken cold pudding can be made fresh again by arranging it in a clean dish and covering it with a meringue.

HEAT THE OVEN PROPERLY FOR CAKES. A layer of sand on the bottom of the oven, about half an inch thick, is a safeguard against burning on the bottom. If the general heat is too great, the cake will burn or crack on the top before it can bake properly; if the oven is not hot enough, the cake will not rise. A safe test of the heat is to put a spoon of the cake dough or batter on a bit of buttered paper and slip it into the oven; the little cake should bake evenly and quickly without burning at the edge.

BAKE DEEP CAKES WITH PAPER. When a cake pan is too shallow for the quantity of cake desired, extend it with stiff glazed paper thickly coated with butter; if the heat is moderate, the butter will preserve the paper from burning.

The Cake Walk

Said the butter to the sugar:
"Will you dance tonight with me, at the cake walk to be given
   in the yellow bowl?
'Twill be the smoothest thing you ever were in before the
   evening's end,
and the swellest, for the Eggs and Baking Powder will attend;
Spring Wheat Flour will come also, and Sweet Milk,
   too will be there—
She's the cream of all the gathering and as rich as she is fair;
and both Nutmeg and Vanilla may come as a special favor,
I hope they will, their presence to the whole thing will add flavor;
tall Granite Spoon will lead us through the dance's mystic maze;
He will take us 'round and 'round in a sort of polonaise.
It's sure to be exclusive and a very fine affair,
for only the most proper of ingredients will be there;
yet it is whispered low that later, after the cake walk turn,
the party altogether to the oven will adjourn;
and if that's true, I'll wager a dollar to a dime
the whole affair will wind up with a very 'hot old time.'"

—Caroline Roberts, Denver,
The Philalethean (Club) Cook Book, 1911

HAVE LIGHTNESS IN MIND WHEN BAKING. Whoever eats heavy pie crust commits a crime against his physical well-being and must pay the penalty. The good housewife should see to it that all pastry and cakes are light; no others should be eaten.

PREPARING THE ICE-CREAM MIXTURE. Ice creams of the most ordinary sort are made of milk thickened with arrowroot or cornstarch in the proportion of a tablespoon to a quart, dissolved in cold water, and boiled in the milk, which is cooled, sweetened, and flavored before it is frozen. The freezing mixture should be composed of three parts of crushed ice to one of coarse salt, and care should be taken that it does not reach high enough around the sides of the can to penetrate to the interior and so spoil the cream.

Introduction of Dr. Price's
HARMLESS FOOD COLORS

There has never been a time like the present, when housekeepers gave so much attention to the apperance as well as to the palatableness of household cookery. ... A love of daintiness is inherent in the heart of every true housewife, and when this can be gained without loss of health or comfort, a great boon has been conferred.

Color schemes enter largely into all forms of entertainment today, and in order to meet these requirements, a fine line of exquisitely prepared liquid colors has been placed on the market by Dr. Price ... to be used fearlessly to color cake, frostings, ices, sherbets, and creams.

LIST OF COLORS:
FRUIT COLORING, STRAWBERRY RED, LEMON YELLOW, CHOCOLATE BROWN, PURPLE VIOLET, BLOOD ORANGE, APPLE GREEN

—*Dr. Price's Delicious Desserts,* 1904

Chapter Twelve

$\mathcal{F}$or the Daily Cook: Family Table Recipes for Breakfast, Luncheon, and Supper

We may live without poetry, music and art,
We may live without conscience, and live without heart;
We may live without friends, we may live without books,
But the civilized man cannot live without cooks.

He may live without books —What is knowledge but grieving?
He may live without hope—What is hope but deceiving?
He may live without love—What is passion but pining?
But where is the man that can live without dining?

—*Good Housekeeping in High Altitudes*, 1888

BREAD AND CEREALS

Southern Corn Bread

Take 1 pint of cornmeal (white); pour ½ pint of boiling water over it, then add a little salt, and with cold water reduce it to the consistency of muffin batter; put in a cool place to rise. If made at night it will be ready to bake for breakfast. If kept in a warm place it will sour. Beat 3 eggs; melt a piece of butter the size of a walnut; lard the size of an egg; a cupful of sweet cream (or milk); a tablespoonful of flour. Grease the pan thoroughly; bake a half hour. The same better can be used for muffins or griddle cakes.

—Mrs. N. Walter Dixon, Pueblo,
The Mesa Workers' Cook Book, 1897

Grand Rapids Rolls

When your bread dough is ready to be made into loaves, cut off a piece about the size of a loaf; add 2 tablespoonsful granulated sugar; 2 tablespoonsful lard; the white of 1 egg beaten light; mould well together; then cut into 12 equal parts, and mould each one thoroughly, and set to rise. When light, bake 20 to 30 minutes a nice rich brown.

—Mrs. Janet S. Harley, Pueblo,
The Mesa Workers' Cook Book, 1897

The Ills of Hot Bread

A peculiarity of our American table, particularly in the Southern and Western States, is the constant exhibition of various preparations of hot bread. In many families of the South and West, bread in loaves to be eaten cold is an article quite unknown. The effect of this kind of diet upon the health has formed a frequent subject of remark among travelers; but only those know the full mischiefs of it who have been compelled to sojourn for a length of time in families where it is maintained. The unknown horrors of dyspepsia from bad bread are a topic over which we willingly draw a veil.

—Harriet Beecher Stowe, *House and Home Papers,* 1869

Denver Biscuit or Rolls

> 1 pint sweet milk scalded and cooled, ½ cup of mashed Irish potatoes, ½ cup sugar, ½ cup lard, ½ cake of Fleishman's yeast cake

While the milk is cooking to milk-warm, take ½ yeast cake and dissolve in ½ cup of lukewarm water. Add to it 1 heaping teaspoonful of baking powder and ½ teaspoonful of soda and potatoes. Beat batter good and set to rise 1 hour, then add to batter ½ cup of lard and 1 tablespoonful of salt. Work flour into this to make a stiff dough, put into a big bowl, grease on top and set away to rise. Let it double in size, then work down, roll out, and cut into biscuits, put into greased pan, and grease on top. Put rest of dough into greased bowl, grease on top. Cover, put into refrigerator, and cut out and cook as you need them. Let the little biscuits rise about 2 hours, then cook in a hot oven. Be sure not to get any of the bread or butter too hot; it will stand a lot of cold, but not heat until you are ready to cook.

—Sarah Ursala (Sallie) Miller (born 1870), from handwritten recipe book of
Lou Annie Miller Almon (born 1866), Decatur, Alabama

Breakfast Menus

Plums and Pears
Corn Meal Mush
Baked Beans   Fish Balls   Brown Bread
Coffee

———

Oatmeal and Heavy Cream
Breakfast Beefsteak with Creamed Potatoes
Buckwheat Cakes   Bacon   Hot Syrup and Melted Butter
Apple Pandowdy with Sweet Cream
Tea, Coffee

—*The Boston Cooking-School Cook Book*, 1896

Pop-overs (for Colorado Altitude)

1 cup milk, 1 cup flour, 2 eggs, ½ teaspoonful salt

These can be made with 1 egg at low altitude. Mix the salt with the flour. Beat the yolks well and add to the milk; then add slowly to the flour to make the batter smooth; then fold in the whites that have been beaten stiff. Fill the hot greased gem pans half full. Bake at once in a hot oven for 30 minutes.

—*The Rocky Mountain Cookbook for High Altitude Cooking*, 1903

Breakfast Tea

Of late, the introduction of English breakfast tea has raised a new sect among the tea-drinkers, reversing some of the old canons. Breakfast tea must be boiled! Unlike the delicate article of olden time, which required only a momentary infusion to develop its richness, this requires a longer and severer treatment to bring out its strength—thus confusing all the established usages, and throwing the work into the hands of the cook in the kitchen. The faults of tea, as too commonly found at our hotels and boarding houses, are that it is made in every way the reverse of what it should be. The water is hot, perhaps, but not boiling; the tea has a general flat, stale, smoky taste, devoid of life or spirit; and it is served, usually, with thin milk, instead of cream. Cream is as essential to the richness of tea as of coffee.

—Harriet Beecher Stowe, *House and Home Papers,* 1869

Ginger Bread

2 cups of sorghum molasses, 1 cup of cool water, ½ cup of butter, 4 cups of Pride of the Rockies Flour, 1 ½ tablespoonsful of ginger, 1 teaspoonful of soda, and 2 well-beaten eggs. Add the molasses to the eggs, then the soda, stirring well, when it foams stir in the other ingredients and bake in a moderate hot oven.

—Mrs. Will Price, Longmont, *The Golden Circle Cook Book,* 1909

Long Island Corn Bread

2 cupsful flour; 1 cupful Indian meal; 2 eggs; butter the size of an egg; 3 tablespoonsful of sugar; 3 teaspoonsful of baking powder; 1 ½ cupsful of milk.

—Mrs. E. T. Gladwin, Pueblo,
The Mesa Workers' Cook Book, 1897

☞

Times are busy with the settler's wife. But during the hay making, and when the threshing and the harvesting begin, then she must be well endowed with those qualities which Dr. Robert Collier sums up under the title of "clear grit" to bear the strain, which is laid upon her. Breakfast takes place by lamp-light, dinner in the fields at noon, and at sundown the men return with the neighbors who have been lending a helping hand—some ten or twelve, perhaps hungry, tired, and dusty, to have their wants supplied. To each must be given a cheerful word of welcome, and for each a plentiful meal must be prepared.

—Brendan MacCarthy, "Home-Life in Colorado,"
in *Catholic World,* December 1884

Hot Mush Bread for Dinner

Scald 1 pint of corn meal until of the consistency of mush; when cooked, cool with sour or buttermilk until about as thick as batter cake dough; then add ½ teaspoonful each of salt and soda, 2 eggs, and 2 teaspoonsful of butter. Beat well and bake quickly. To be served in the dish in which it is baked, and helped with a spoon.

—Mrs. Cooper, Leadville, *Cloud City Cook-Book,* 1899

Rusk

2 pints milk and 2 pints sugar; warm slightly, add ½ cup yeast, raisins, and some flour. Let set overnight, and in the morning add salt, 3 beaten eggs, 2 heaping cups melted butter, and more flour. Let is rise, then make into rolls, and when light, bake.

—Mrs. O. H. Simons, Leadville, *Cloud City Cook-Book,* 1889

Jellies and Jams

Grape Preserves

Wash the grapes, weigh, having equal weight of sugar and grapes; then pulp the grapes, put the pulp in a kettle and boil 25 minutes. Rub through a sieve; return this to the kettle, add the sugar, and boil 30 minutes, then put in the skins and boil 10 minutes.

—Miss R. H. Nash, Leadville,
Cloud City Cook-Book, 1899

Raspberry Shrub

1 quart vinegar to 3 quarts berries; place in a jar for one night, then add 1 pound sugar to each pint of the liquid, and boil ½ hour; when cool bottle, seal and put in a cool place.

—Mrs. Hoskin, Denver,
The Twenty-Third Avenue Presbyterian Cook Book, 1897

The Most Economical Breakfast Dish (Beautiful Also)

Keep a jar for remnants of bread, both coarse and fine, potatoes, remnants of hominy, rice, grits, cracked wheat, oatmeal, and all other articles used on the table. Add all remnants of milk, whether sour or sweet, and water enough to soak all, so as to be soft, but not thin. When enough is collected, add enough water to make a batter for griddle cakes and put in enough soda to sweeten it. Add 2 spoonsful of sugar, ½ a teaspoonful of salt, and 2 eggs for each quart, and you make an excellent dish of material, most of it usually wasted. Thicken it a little with fine flour, and it makes fine waffles.

—*Miss Beecher's Housekeeper and Healthkeeper,* 1873

THE DAILY MENU

Colorado Springs, November 1871

"The food is good and plentiful. Beefsteak or venison; biscuit—as they call hot rolls out here; hot buckwheat cakes eaten with butter and molasses or honey; and the whole washed down with bad tea or excellent rich milk.

Colorado Springs, November 30, 1871

Mrs. S., who is cooking at a log cabin for the men working on the house, gave us a capital dinner, off tin plates; and taught me how to make biscuit, which means hot rolls, and slap-jacks, a kind of pancakes which one eats at breakfast and tea, in a little pile, covered with butter and syrup, or honey.

—*South by West or Winter in the Rocky Mountains and Spring in Mexico*, 1874

MEAT STUFFS

French Beef: A Charming Breakfast Dish

Take 1 pound of lean, tender beef; remove every particle of fat from it and scrape it up with a very sharp knife into a perfect pulp; then with a knife and fork mince the pulp still finer. Put it in a sauce pan with salt and pepper to taste, 1 tablespoonful of cold water, 2 tablespoonsful of rich sweet cream, a piece of butter the size of an egg; set on stove to cook, stirring constantly; when it has been cooking a minute or two, but still looks rare, stir in 1 tablespoonful of cracker dust and 1 tablespoon-ful of mixed mustard. If you have no cracker dust, cream 1 teaspoonful of flour with butter and stir in. Stir well and let cook a minute or two, but not too long or it will be spoiled. Take it up while it is yet slightly rare, or at least just done. Garnish with parsley.

—*How We Cook in Colorado*, 1907

Breakfast Dish

Take kidney; soak in salt water with a little baking soda; wash in fresh water and cut away all the fat; put on in cold water to boil; after it has boiled until tender take the kidney and cut in thin slices; strain the broth and put the kidney in; set away till morning as kidney should be cooked the day before using; then let it come to a boil in morning; thicken with a few tablespoonsful of corn starch; salt and pepper to taste. A little salt should be added when cooking the first time.

—Mrs. J. Walters, Denver, *The Twenty-Third Avenue Presbyterian Cook Book*, 1897

Scraple

One-half hog's head soaked overnight in salt water, cut out eyes and ears. Boil till meat leaves the bones; chop meat fine; 3 pounds liver, boiled, chopped fine. Save water the head is boiled in. Add 1 gallon water more; put in meat and liver; add salt, pepper, and sage to taste; thicken with equal parts of buckwheat, cornmeal, and flour, as stiff as mush. Cut in slices when cold, and fry brown like mush.

—Mrs. L. J. Taylor, Pueblo, *The Mesa Workers' Cook Book,* 1897

Tongue on Toast

Cut cold boiled tongue into dice; put it into a saucepan with a table-spoonful of butter, ½ teacup of stock, ½ teaspoonful of salt, pepper, or cayenne to taste, and 2 beaten eggs; stir over the fire until the mixture becomes thick, but do not allow it to reach even the bubbling point, or it will curdle. Serve on toast.

—I. B., Denver,
The Twenty-Third Avenue Presbyterian Cook Book, 1897

Veal Loaf

¾ pound raw veal, ¼ pound raw salt-pork, 3 eggs, 9 crackers, 3 tea-spoonsful salt, 1 ½ teaspoonsful pepper, parsley. Chop very fine, and bake 1 hour. When cold, slice and serve.

—Mrs. W. H. Nash, Leadville, *Cloud City Cook-Book,* 1889

Veal Stew

Take 3 or 4 pounds of the breast of veal; cut in pieces about 2 inches thick; put in a stewpan with 1 ½ quarts of boiling water; remove the scum as fast as it arises; when it is all removed cover closely and let simmer till tender; season with salt, a slice of onion, and a little pepper. Take 8 or 10 potatoes, cut in halves the longest way, put in the stew, and boil till tender, but do not allow them to boil to pieces; when done, take up the hot meat on a platter in shape of a mound; place the halves of potatoes around it, one about the other, nearly to the top; make a gravy of the liquor that remains in the kettle, adding in more water, if needed, with a ½ lump of butter; thicken with flour; pour 2 or 3 tablespoonsful of gravy over the top and interedge with sprigs of parsley; serve the remainder of the gravy in a gravy dish. This makes a pretty, palatable, and inexpensive dish. Mutton and lamb may be used in the same way. Yellow turnips may be boiled in the same pot, cut in round, thin slices, and garnish the outer edge of the platter with a row of parsley between them and the potato.

—F. S., Denver, *The Twenty-Third Avenue Presbyterian Cook Book*, 1897

Chicken Noodles

Stew one chicken, disjointing it. Take 5 eggs and beat very light. Knead with flour until very stiff, then roll very thin and cut in fine shreds. Cook 10 minutes and thicken with a little flour and milk.

—Mrs. E. D. Sommers, Colorado Springs, *Good Housekeeping in High Altitudes*, 1888

Stewed Venison

Cut it into steaks, spread over them a thin layer of stuffing made with bread crumbs, minced onion, parsley, pepper, salt, and a little pork chopped fine; now roll them separately and tie them each with a cord; stew them in boiling water or stock. Thicken the gravy with flour and butter mixed and add 1 or 2 spoonsful of sherry or port wine.

—Mrs. Henderson, Denver, *Our Kitchen Friend*, 1889

Luncheon Menus

Turkey Soup   Veal Loaf   Lettuce Salad
Bavarian Cream

—The Enterprising Housekeeper, 1898

Beef Stew with Dumplings
Sliced Oranges   Cake   Tea

—The Boston Cooking-School Cook Book, 1896

Green Pea Soup with Diced Salt Pork.
Boiled Ham and Egg Sauce.
Potato Croquettes & Escalloped Tomatoes.
Homemade Bread and Freshly Churned Butter.
Coleslaw.   Pickles, sweet 'n sour.   Pudding & Pie.

—Custer County Women's Club

Pigeon Pie

Make a fine puff paste, lay a border of it around a large dish, and cover the bottom with a veal cutlet or a very tender steak free from fat and bone; season with salt, cayenne pepper, and mace. Prepare as many pigeons as can be put in one layer in the dish, put in each pigeon a small lump of butter, and season with pepper and salt; lay them in the dish breast downward and cut in slices a half dozen of hard-boiled eggs and lay in with the birds; put in more butter, some veal broth, and cover the whole with crust. Bake slowly for 1 ½ hour.

—Mrs. L., Denver, *Our Kitchen Friend,* 1889

Luncheon, as the mid-day meal in the ordinary household, is far too often an indifferent affair... Luncheon is, in many places, peculiarly the woman's meal, and for this very reason sufficient care and thought should be expended upon it to tempt the delicate appetite and give the needed nourishment in an attractive form.

Relishes are nowhere more acceptable than upon the luncheon table, but that which deserves the highest consideration for this meal is the utilization of culinary odds and ends. Croquettes, soufflés, meats for sandwiches, and all meat entrées become simplified by means of a meat chopper, and the majority of dishes coming under the head of entrées are but different forms of hash or minced meat.

—*The Enterprising Housekeeper,* 1898

At 2 p.m. lunch

I commonly invite to that—cup of tea and biscuit and butter with cold meat—any gentleman I wish to have more conference with than is practicable in hours given to miscellaneous business.

—President Rutherford B. Hayes,
White House Diary, March 18, 1878

VEGETABLES, TOO

Many of these dishes will serve you just as well at breakfast, luncheon, supper, or dinner.

Colorado Springs Baked Beans

Soak 1 quart of beans overnight. In the morning parboil in plenty of water half or three-quarters of an hour after the skin cracks open. If hard to cook, add ½ teaspoonful of soda. Drain and put in bean pot with a piece of pork half as large as your hand, 2 tablespoonsful of molasses, 1 teaspoonful of salt, cover with hot water. Let them remain in the oven until noon the next day with no extra fire during the night.

—Mrs. G. H. Stone, Colorado Springs, *Good Housekeeping in High Altitudes*, 1888

Corn Oysters

Grate the corn from 6 ears, salt and pepper to taste; add 1 beaten egg, ¼ cup of melted butter, 2 crackers, powdered fine; fry in butter on a hot griddle. If the consistency is not right to fry, add a little flour.

—*How We Cook in Colorado*, 1907

Squash Pies

2 cups squash boiling hot, 2 cups boiling milk. Stir well, cool, and sift. Add 1 cup cold milk, or ½ cup each milk and cream, 2 eggs, sugar and salt, and cinnamon to taste. Bake with rich under crust.

—Mrs. E. C. Bartlett, Colorado Springs, *Good Housekeeping in High Altitudes*, 1888

Population claimed, six thousand. I am sorry to cut them down to four thousand, but that is more than they can count, unless they add the flies, of which at least several millions dine with us every day.

—*From the Atlantic to the Pacific, Overland Via the Overland Stage,* 1865

Celery Root

Pare and boil about 30 minutes in salted water; thicken the liquor with flour and cream or milk; salt and pepper to taste; pour over toast.

—I. B., Denver, *The Twenty-Third Avenue Presbyterian Cook Book,* 1897

Supper Menus

Broiled Tomatoes   Potato Croquettes
Peach Shortcake   Chocolate

—*The Enterprising Housekeeper,* 1898

Creamed Chicken & Biscuits.   Cold Sliced Ham.
Baked Potatoes & Succotash.   Pickles and Spiced Peaches.
Cake and Ice Cream.

—Custer County Women's Club

EGGS & CHEESE

Macaroni and Cheese

Break ¼ pound macaroni in pieces; cook in boiling water until soft; put a layer in bottom of a greased bake dish; upon this a layer of cracker crumbs; then grated cheese and tiny bits of butter; season with ground mustard and salt; continue in this way until dish is filled, with grated cheese on top; wet with milk and bake 20 or 30 minutes.

—Miss McClung, Denver, *The Twenty-Third Avenue Presbyterian Cook Book,* 1897

Nuns Toast

Slice 4 or 5 hard-boiled eggs. Put a piece of butter in a saucepan and when it begins to bubble add some finely chopped celery, a cup of milk into which a teaspoonful of flour has been stirred, and stir until smooth and hot. Add the slices of egg, season, and pour over buttered toast.

—Mrs. M. S. Crawford , Colorado Springs, *Good Housekeeping in High Altitudes,* 1888

Egg Balls

Boil 4 eggs hard; take out the yolks and pound them; add 2 table-spoonsful of bread crumbs; mix the yolk of 1 raw egg; take the whites and pound them; mix all in long rolls; fry or boil in water 2 minutes. Serve with toast.

—Mrs. Emerson, Denver, *The Twenty-Third Avenue Presbyterian Cook Book,* 1897

Supper as the evening meal, has quietly accepted the neglected corner into which it has been thrust. ... Except in the heat of summer, a hot dish should always be served for supper. ... Soups are rarely served. Shellfish served raw or cooked in any form; small fish, broiled or fried; broiled steaks, chops, or chicken—all these are acceptable, especially when a hearty supper is required. But here, as with luncheon, made-over dishes are most often used. Potatoes, rice, hominy, and tomatoes in special forms, such as croquettes, scallops, etc., are served; other vegetables rarely, if ever. Eggs, salads, sandwiches in any form, hot breads, griddle cakes, and waffles—all these belong to supper. ...

—*The Enterprising Housekeeper*, 1898

Egg Sauce

Take 3 hard-boiled eggs and a good teacupful of drawn butter. Chop the yolks very fine and beat into the hot drawn butter, salting to taste. This is used for boiled fowls and boiled fish. For the former, you can add some minced parsley, for the latter, chopped pickles or capers.

—*Our Kitchen Friend*, 1899

Egg Salad

Take hard-boiled eggs, cut in half after removing the shell, pulverize the yolks, moisten with vinegar, add salt, pepper, celery seed, and mustard, mix well, place back into the whites. Good to serve with lettuce.

—Mrs. P. C. Cronkite, Denver, *How We Cook in Colorado*, 1907

Oyster Omelette

To ½ cupful cream add 6 eggs beaten very lightly; season with salt and pepper and pour into frying pan with tablespoonful butter. Drop in a dozen large oysters and fry light brown. Double over and serve hot.

—Mrs. E. F. Gladwin, Pueblo, *The Mesa Workers' Cook Book*, 1897

SALADS

Salmon Salad

1 pound can of salmon, 3 hard-boiled eggs, 2 large lemons, and 8 tablespoonsful of vinegar. Mix well the salmon, vinegar, and juice of 1 lemon. Slice 1 egg and 1 lemon and mix carefully. Garnish with lettuce leaves and the 2 hard-boiled eggs sliced. Use the oil of salmon or olive oil, according to taste.

—Mrs. W. F. McKeehan, Colorado Springs, *Good Housekeeping in High Altitudes*, 1888

Salad to Serve with Game

A good salad to serve with game is made of acid oranges, walnuts, and watercress. Peel the oranges and remove all the white skin; slice them very thin, cutting down the sides instead of across the fruit; arrange them in two rows on a flat dish and scatter walnut meats over them. On either side of the slices and through the center place rows of watercress. Make a dressing of 2 tablespoonsful of lemon juice and 4 of olive oil; season with salt and cayenne pepper and pour over the salad. Place the dish in the refrigerator, so that the salad may be very cold when served.

—"Fancy Cook," Pueblo, *The Mesa Workers' Cook Book*, 1897

Celery Salad

1 pint of white cabbage, chopped; ½ pint of chopped celery (or more celery and less cabbage, if you like); 9 tablespoonsful of vinegar; 1 ounce butter; ¼ teaspoonful of mustard; 1 teaspoonful of salt; a pinch

of cayenne pepper; 1 tablespoonful of sugar, and the yolks of 2 eggs; mix mustard, eggs, sugar, salt and pepper together, then add butter and vinegar; put it on the stove, and stir constantly until it thickens; let it cool, and when cold add 3 tablespoonsful of sweet cream; pour this over the cabbage and celery; if not moist enough a little more vinegar may be added. A nice salad can be made of cabbage, using celery vinegar, if the celery cannot be obtained.

—Mrs. M. S. Donaldson, Denver,
The Twenty-Third Avenue Presbyterian Cook Book, 1897

Let's Have a Little Joy Ride

... in the Underwood fairy-land, where everything is in "good taste" and everybody says "Taste the taste."

Here goes for the ride. Hold on tight or you may get spilled at the curves.

To the Waldorf went one of the newly rich; in search of good taste was he. Unable to understand the "manoo," he said unto the waiter, "Bring me $25 worth of ham and eggs." Ham was the best taste he knew—wise raw recruit of the newly rich.

And when you really think it over, is there any taste that actually does taste as good as ham? There is not.

And, in sooth, what could make a taster taste tastier than good boiled ham and 42 spices all ground up fine? That's what Underwood Deviled Ham is, and that's one reason why it tastes good.

However, all ham hasn't the said described taste. Some hams taste good and some taste punk.

But Underwood Ham has the taste—the home ham taste that you got from the farm-cured hams of your girlhood "on the old Brandywine."

—*Taste the Taste and Some Cookery News*, by W.M. Underwood Co.,
"First Canners in America," 52 Fulton Street, Boston

Decorative Salads from the Ladies
of Pueblo's Mesa Presbyterian Church

Mrs. Bradford's Pond-Lily Egg Salad

Remove the shells from hard-boiled eggs, and beginning at the small end of each egg cut the whites lengthwise into fifths almost to the base, taking care to leave the yolks whole. Turn back the "petals" thus formed, so as to make each egg simulate an open pond-lily. Roughen the surface of the yolks with a fork. The petals can be colored pale pink by using a small soft paint brush dipped in beet juice. Place the "lilies" on lettuce leaves on a shallow dish, and serve with mayonnaise or French dressing, and bread and butter crisps.

Mrs. George E. Gray's Cress and Egg Salad

Dress a bunch of cress with oil, vinegar, salt, and paprika. Cut the whites of 2 hard-boiled eggs into 8 lengthwise pieces and arrange them on the cress to simulate the petals of a flower. Press a star of mayonnaise dressing in the center of the petal. Pass an egg yolk through a sieve and arrange around the dressing. Send to the table in this form, but toss together when serving.

Bird's Nest Salad

Take spinach that has been cooked and drained, and while hot press some of the leaves with a spoon in a bowl to obtain a green liquid; strain this through a fine sieve; rub enough of this liquid with some black pepper into Philadelphia cream cheese to give it a delicate green color. Roll this paste into balls the size of robins' eggs. With clean sharp scissors cut crisp lettuce leaves into shreds and make them into nests upon a pretty platter or shallow dish. Into each nest place 5 eggs. Pass in some pretty dish, mayonnaise or French dressing. Serve cheese straws with this salad.

—The Mesa Workers' Cook Book, 1897

Artistry of Salads

It looks so dainty, so tempting,
So fit for the taste of a queen,
Such epicurean colors,
Such garnishings of green,
Such art! But I turn from it bravely,
I dare not do more than to look,
For I know were I only to taste it,
I should fall in love with the cook.

—How We Cook in Colorado, 1907

Summer Menu

And the offerings [of summer] arrive with such glorious progressiveness! First comes the strawberry, like a blush on the cheek of Mother Earth; then the berries and vegetables of more vigorous growth; then the stately, luscious melon, the charm and glory of the breakfast table; then corn, which is meat in nutrition; with the juicy apple, the pride of prince and peasant. Then we come to the pear and to the orchard—

Where peaches grow with sunny dyes,
Like maiden's cheeks when blushes rise,
Where huge figs the branches bend.
Where clusters from the vine distend.
There is the feast which nature spreads.
Let every man say grace in his heart and partake of it thankfully.

—Dr. Chase's Third Last and Complete Receipt Book
and Household Physician, 1903

Some Things that Can Be Served with a Salad

Nut, cheese, olive, pickle, nasturtium, lettuce, watercress, cucumber, ginger, mint, and plain sandwiches made from all kinds of bread, rolls, and crackers. Different kinds of cheese, either toasted or plain, served with crackers or bread-and-butter sandwiches, cheese soufflé, frozen cheese, cheese croquettes, cheese balls, and cheese in any palatable form, is permissible with salads. Wine or orange jelly moulded with nuts or fruits, or plain, is very delicious served with a salad.

RADISH ROSES For these use the small, round ones. Cut the radish in scallops in two layers. Soak in ice water 2 hours before serving.

RADISH TULIPS Select small ones of oblong shape, cut them in quarters nearly down to the stem. Soak.

—*The Rocky Mountain Cookbook for High Altitude Cooking,* 1903

CHAPTER THIRTEEN

RECIPES FOR DINNER:
SOUPS AND MEATS

SOUPS

Economical Soup

Gather up the fragments that remain that nothing be lost. John, vi, 12.

Use the bones and cold pieces of roast beef or steak which have been left over; put over to boil slowly in 2 or 3 quarts of water, according to quantity of meat; cover the kettle to prevent to rapid evaporation; cook 2 hours; add 2 or 3 potatoes, 1 turnip, 1 carrot, 1 onion; salt and pepper to taste; bring to boil, then remove to back of stove where it will simmer slowly for 5 or 6 hours; strain through colander; return to soup kettle and thicken with a little flour made smooth in cold water;

add celery, salt, and 1 cup of cold boiled rice; serve small cubes of toasted stale bread with this soup.

—Mrs. C. H. Emmons, Denver, *How We Cook in Colorado*, 1907

Black Bean Soup

1 pint of beans soaked overnight in 1 gallon of water (cold). ½ pound of pork, same of beef, 1 or 2 onions, 2 small carrots grated. Pepper and salt. When done, strain the soup through a colander; wine and hard-boiled eggs added are a great improvement. It may be made without any meat and simple seasoned like any other bean soup. Never use pork.

—Mrs. Vroom, Denver, *Our Kitchen Friend*, 1889

Mulligatawny

3 quarts stock; 2 sour apples; 2 onions; 2 tablespoonsful butter; 2 teaspoonsful curry powder; 2 teaspoonsful salt; 2 tablespoonsful flour; 2 tablespoonsful desiccated cocoanut; juice of 1 lemon; put butter into kettle and melt; add the apple and onion sliced; fry together 10 minutes, then add the flour, curry powder, and cocoanut; stir in butter while off stove; then add stock; allow to simmer on stove until onion and apple are tender; add salt; rub the whole through sieve; return to the stove, and when it comes to a boil it is ready to be served with rice.

—Mrs. Frank L. Morey, Denver, *The Twenty-Third Avenue Presbyterian Cook Book*, 1897

Soup rejoices the stomach and disposes it to receive other foods.

—*How We Cook in Colorado*, 1907

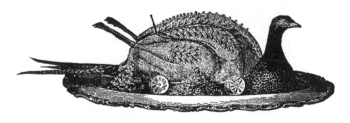

DINNER MEATS

Possum and Sweet Potatoes

Pour a large kettleful of hot water into a convenient vessel, add a small shovelful of ashes and then put the 'possum in; turn the 'possum round until fur is loosened, and it can easily be scraped clean. Draw, remove head and feet, wash thoroughly, salt in and outside, let hang over night to freeze. Wash again and put in baking pan with a little water; cover closely and put over the fire. When tender, remove cover and put in oven to brown. Dust with pepper and baste frequently with drippings; have medium potatoes peeled and boiled tender in slightly salted water, adding butter and a little sugar. When tender, arrange potatoes around 'possum, basting frequently with juices until brown. Arrange 'possum on hot platter with potatoes round him, and serve.

—*Holland's Cook Book,* 1926

Curried Oysters

1 quart of oysters, 1 teaspoonful of curry powder, 1 teaspoonful of flour, 1 of butter, salt and pepper to taste. Cook the oysters in their own liquor over a slow fire, add salt and pepper, butter and curry powder, rubbed smooth. When the oysters are firm, moisten the flour with water to make a paste, and thicken the liquor. It must be watched carefully and stirred thoroughly, after adding flour and water. The rise to be boiled separately and put all around the edge of the dish.

—Mrs. Kilgour, Denver, *Our Kitchen Friend,* 1889

The Frenchman, who locks the door of his shop from 12:30 till 2 o'clock, so as not to be disturbed by customers while he is having his dinner with his wife and a good time with the children, I say, this man has solved the great problem, the only problem of life, happiness, far better than the American who, at one o'clock, will stick at his door: "Gone to dinner; shall be back in five minutes." Five minutes to dinner, just think of it! The greatest event of the day. And what is the result of that five minutes to dinner in America? The result is that the whole continent, from New York to San Francisco, from British Columbia to Louisiana, cities, forests, prairies, the whole landscape, is spoiled, made an eyesore of, by the advertisements of liver pills.

—Max O'Rell, "Studies in Cheerfulness," in *The North American Review*, December 1898

"Little Pigs in Blankets"

Take large oysters, wrap each one in a slice of bacon cut very thin, fasten with little wooden skewers, fry quickly in a hot spider, and serve on toast.

—Mrs. Beardsley, Denver, *Our Kitchen Friend*, 1889

Calves Brains

Before cooking, remove all the fibrous membrane, then throw them into a pint of cold water in which are mixed ½ teaspoonful of salt and 1 teaspoonful of vinegar; boil 3 minutes, then plunge them into cold water. Cut them into scallops, and when seasoned with pepper and salt, egged and breadcrumbed, fry in a little hot butter.

—Mrs. A. H. Estes, Denver, *How We Cook in Colorado*, 1907

How to Prepare Beaver Tail

Where good beaver tail on table, push everything else back!
—Colorado Frontiersman

Scald well; with a knife scrape off the black scales. Singe the hairs. Cook in heavy black kettle till tender, pouring off the water several times. Remove meat from tailbone. Meat is white and gelatinous. It may be used in a number of ways:

☞ Serve whole on platter with lemon and butter sauce.

☞ Cut into cubes and add to navy been soup. Salt and pepper generously.

☞ Pack cooked beaver tail in a crock, cover with hot pickling brine and let stand several hours. Pickling beaver tail is especially good to disguise the strong flavor if beaver have been eating too many willows.

—Margaret Emerine Bourn Crawford (Mrs. James H.), resident of Colorado from 1863, Founders of Steamboat Springs

Roast Chicken

Cover the breast of the fowl or chicken with butter or drippings or better still tie a piece of fat bacon over it, place in a bag and set on broiler in a hot oven, allow 25 minutes for a small spring chicken, 35 minutes for a large fowl, 45 to 50 minutes according to size for stuffed poultry or game in a moderate oven.

—Mr. Soyer, Denver, *The Philalethean (Club) Cook Book*, 1911

☞ *Colorado Springs, November 1871*

We pulled up at a log cabin by the side of the track, and from the door-way came a voice, saying, "Dinner's on the table." Out we all got, and I thought—Surely we can't be going to dine in this place: but... I found, to my amazement... clean linen, smart waiters, and a first-rate dinner; far better than any we had had on the Kansas Pacific. I was in a state of complete bewilderment; but hunger soon got the better of surprise, and we did ample justice to oyster-soup and roast antelope.

—*South by West or Winter in the Rocky Mountains and Spring in Mexico*, 1874

Roasted Rabbits

Skin and dress the rabbits as soon as possible and hang them overnight; roast them before a moderate fire, basting them with butter and a little flour when nearly done.

—*Our Kitchen Friend*, 1889

Sauer Kraut with Oysters

Drain the oysters. Mix some flour with part of the liquor, put the rest of the liquor on the stove, let come to a boil; add oysters and flour and let come to a boil again; add pepper and salt and piece of butter. Then fill dish with layer of sauer kraut and layer of oysters alternately. Serve at once.

—Mrs. Werner, Leadville, *Cloud City Cook Book*, 1899

November 7, 1866

George shot two rabbits this morning & we had them for dinner. Vatie (8-year-old daughter) said, "Poor fellows! They were so happy this morning."

Amelia Butts (Mrs. George) Buss, *Diary*, 1866-1867

Serving Fresh Meat

The faults in the meat generally furnished to us are, first, that it is too new. A beefsteak, which three or four days of keeping might render practicable, is served up to us palpitating with freshness, with all the toughness of animal muscle yet warm.

In the Western country, the traveler, on approaching a hotel, is often saluted by the last shrieks of the chickens which half an hour afterward are presented to him a la spread-eagle for his dinner.

—Harriet Beecher Stowe, *House and Home Papers*, 1869

Dinner Menus

Macaroni Soup
Fricassee of Lamb   Riced Potatoes   Stewed Tomatoes
String Bean and Radish Salad   Fruit and Nuts

Cream of Celery Soup
Roast Beef   Franconia Potatoes   Yorkshire Pudding
Macaroni with Cheese   Tomato and Lettuce Salad
Chocolate Cream   Café Noir

Duchess Soup
Fried Fillets of Halibut   Shredded Potatoes   Hot Slaw
Beefsteak Pie
Irish Moss Blanc-Mange with Vanilla Wafers

—*The Boston Cooking-School Cook Book,* 1896

Spring Soup
Broiled Beefsteak   Royal Croquettes
Mashed Potatoes   Parsnips with Cream Sauce
Lettuce with Mayonnaise Dressing
Minnie's Lemon Pie   Nuts and Raisins

—*Ransom's Family Receipt Book,* 1885

CHAPTER FOURTEEN

RECIPES FOR DESSERTS AND BEVERAGES

DESSERTS

One Family's Dessert Recipes

CREAM TARTER CAKE 1 pint flour, 1 cup sweet milk, 1 cup sugar, 1 egg, 2 ½ teaspoonsful butter, 1 teaspoonful soda, a teaspoonsful cream.

BREAD CAKE 4 cups bread, 1 ½ cups butter, 2 cups sugar, 2 eggs, 1 spoonful of saleratus and cinnamon.

SUGAR CAKE 2 cups sugar, ⅔ cups butter, 7 cups flour. Rub flour and butter together. Then put in sugar, ½ pint water, 1 teaspoonful hartshorn (or ½ soda, 1 cream tartar). Let stand 2 hours and roll thin.

QUICK SPONGE CAKE 1 cup sugar, 1 cup flour well mixed with 1 teaspoonful of cream tartar and ½ saleratus, break in 3 eggs to the sugar and flour. Flavor with lemon, ½ cup of cream, or 2 tablespoonsful of butter.

SOFT GINGER CAKE 1 cup sugar, 1 cup butter, 1 cup sour milk, 1 cup molasses, 4 eggs, 4 cups flour, 2 teaspoonsful saleratus, 1 tablespoonful ginger. Stir butter and sugar to cream. Put saleratus in.

☛

Trail Pie

September 11, 1866

There has been cacktus or prickly pear all a long the road today. The buds on them are good to eat & some make pies of them. They are about the size of a butternut & have a pleasant sour taste.

—Amelia Butts (Mrs. George) Buss,
Diary, 1866-1867

COFFEE CAKE 1 ½ cups molasses, 1 cup sugar, ⅔ cups butter, 1 cup coffee, 1 teaspoonful of soda, cinnamon, 2 cloves.

ECONOMICAL PUDDING Keep your pieces of bread, and dry them nice when enough are collected, soak them in milk overnight; in the morning drain out all the milk you can through a cullender; add to the bread some sugar and a little salt, with some scalded raisins; tie it in a bag, and boil 5 or 6 hours. Serve with sweet sauce.

PLAIN BAKED BREAD PUDDING Pound rusked bread fine; to 5 heaping tablespoonsful of it put 1 quart milk, 3 beaten eggs, 3 tablespoonsful rolled sugar, 1 teaspoonful salt, ½ nutmeg, and 3 tablespoonsful melted butter. Bake about an hour.

STEAM PUDDING 1 cup sour milk, 1 teaspoonful cream tartar, ½ teaspoonful soda, 2 eggs, 1 teaspoonful saleratus. Steam 1 hour.

—*Darley Family Papers,*
186?

Ice Cream and Ices from the Ladies of Pueblo's Mesa Presbyterian Church

Laura Wilson's Ice Cream

Take 2 quarts new milk. Put on 3 pints to boil in a custard kettle or a pail set within a kettle of boiling water. Beat the yolks and whites of 4 eggs separately. (As many as 8 eggs may be used, but I prefer 4). Mix the yolks with the remaining pint and stir slowly into the boiling milk. Boil 2 minutes; remove from the stove; immediately add 1 ½ pounds sugar; let it dissolve; strain while hot through a crash towel; cool; add 1 quart rich cream and 2 tablespoonsful vanilla (or season to taste, remembering that the strength of the flavoring, also the sweetness, is very much diminished by the freezing). Set the custard and also the whites (not beaten) in a cool place until needed. In about 3 hours before serving begin the preparations for freezing. Prepare the freezer by making a compact mass of small pieces of ice, interlaid with coarse salt around it. Then pour the custard, to which you have just added the well-whipped whites, into the freezer, filling ⅔ full to give room for expansion. Then freeze.

Nanna Jaerner's Peach Ice Cream

3 pounds ripe peaches; cut and mash and put through colander; sweeten peaches to taste; 1 pint cream; 1 quart milk; beat 2 eggs and stir with other ingredients. Freeze until hard.

Mrs. E. O. Nash's Lemon Ice

To 2 quarts water add the juice of 6 lemons and 1 ½ pounds granulated sugar. When partly frozen stir in the whites of 2 eggs, beaten stiff.

—*The Mesa Workers' Cook Book*, 1897

Sherbets from the Ladies of the First Baptist Church, Denver

Mrs. N. M. Tabor's Orange Sherbet

½ pound granulated sugar, 3 eggs, the whites only, 1 ⅕ pints of water, ⅕ teaspoon cream of tartar, juice of 3 oranges; boil the sugar and water to a thin syrup and let cool; beat eggs very stiff and add the cream of tartar, stirring for 5 minutes; strain the orange juice also syrup through a fine strainer into the freezer, then add the eggs.

Mrs. I. B. Porter's Pineapple Sherbet

2 cans of pineapples, 3 lemons, 4 eggs, whites only; put the pineapple on the stove with 1 pint of boiling water and cook until tender. Chop fine, mash, and strain with the juice of 3 lemons. Take 2 cups of sugar and boil with water until it is a thick syrup; stir it into the juice of the pine apple and lemon; add the whites of the eggs well beaten, freeze.

Miss Coburn's Lemon Sherbet

5 lemons, 1 pint sugar, 1 quart water, 1 tablespoonful gelatine, dissolved; heat all together and freeze when cold.

Mrs. G. A. Gano's Strawberry Sherbet

The juice of 1 quart of strawberries, 1 ½ pints of water, 1 pint of sugar, whites of 4 eggs; stir all together and freeze.

Roosevelt Cakes

Cut rich white cake in squares; cut the squares in halves and spread with apricot jam; cover with the other half. Press whipped cream through a pastry bag in fanciful shapes on top, or if the bag is not used, dot with the cream and sprinkle with finely-cut angelica.

—*The Rocky Mountain Cookbook for High Altitude Cooking*, 1903

✸ **HARD SAUCE No. 2.** Cream 1 cup butter and 2 cups sugar, and flavor to taste.

✸ **GOOD SAUCE.** Beat 1 cup sugar and ½ cup butter to a cream; add 1 egg beaten well, ½ cup wine, and 3 tablespoonsful water. Stir well and set it over a boiling teakettle a few minutes before serving.

✸ **VERY NICE SAUCE.** Beat the yolk of 1 egg with ½ cup white sugar and a tablespoon of cornstarch; stir in 3 tablespoonsful boiling water; set it over a teakettle to keep warm. Just as you take it to the table, stir in lightly the white of egg beaten with other ½ cup of sugar, a little nutmeg, and a spoonful of brandy or wine.

✸ **CONFEDERATE SAUCE FOR CAKE.** 2 cups sugar, 1 tablespoonful butter, yolk of 1 egg beaten well. Mix well and pour in ¼ pint of boiling milk; add a glass of wine and season with nutmeg.

—*The Capitol Cook Book,* 1899

Colorado Cake

2 cups sugar, ½ cup butter, 1 cup milk, 3 level cups flour, 5 eggs, 3 squares of Bakers' chocolate melted, 2 teaspoonsful of cinnamon, 1 of the cloves and nutmeg, 1 teaspoonful vanilla, 2 teaspoonsful baking powder, ½ cup chopped walnuts put in the batter. Put 1 cup of nuts in filling.

—Mrs. Arthur Bender, Longmont,
The Golden Circle Cook Book, 1909

Rocky Mountain Cake (Loaf or Layer Cake)

1 scant cup of sugar, ½ cup of butter, ½ teaspoonful of baking powder, ¼ teaspoonful of salt, ½ cut of milk, 3 eggs, 1 ¾ cups of flour.

Flavoring: Cream the butter and sugar, add flavoring of any kind, the well-beaten eggs, part of the flour (with the salt and baking powder sifted in it), the milk and the rest of the flour; beat thoroughly for 10 minutes. Bake in gem pans if you like.

—*The Rocky Mountain Cookbook for High Altitude Cooking,* 1903

Cottage Cheese Pie

4 egg yolks; 2 cups cottage cheese, sieved; ½ cup seedless raisins; ⅛ teaspoonful salt; 1 ½ cups sugar; 1 cup thin cream; juice of ½ lemon and grated rind; 2 egg whites, beaten.

Beat yolks slightly, add sugar, cheese, cream, raisins, lemon, salt and stir well. Then fold in whites of 2 eggs. Pour into a pie plate lined with pastry and bake at 450° for 10 minutes. Reduce heat to 325° and bake for 20 more minutes.

—Augusta Hauck Block (Mrs. Joseph H.),
Crested Butte and Denver, born in 1872

Denver Pound Cake

½ pound butter, ½ pound powdered sugar, 5 eggs, grater rind of ½ lemon, ½ pound flour.

Break the eggs one at a time in a large plate and beat with the hand. Then beat in the butter and sugar that have been creamed together. Add the flour and the lemon juice. Bake for 1 hour.

—*The Rocky Mountain Cook Book for High Altitude Cooking,* 1903

Hominy Cake

1 pint of boiled hominy, 1 pint of sweet milk, 3 eggs, 1 tablespoonful butter, salt to taste, 1 teacup of flour; bake in a dripping pan. Be sure not to use any soda or baking powder.

—Mrs. Driscot, Denver,
Our Kitchen Friend, 1889

Molasses Layer Cake

1 cup molasses; yolk of 1 egg; 1 tablespoonful butter; 1 teaspoonful cloves; 1 teaspoonful cinnamon. Stir as thick as possible with flour; then add 1 cup boiling water and 1 teaspoonful soda. Bake in four layers.

Filling: white of 1 egg; 1 cupful sugar, boiled as for icing. Then stir in white of egg and ½ cupful raisins (seeded), chopped fine.

—Mrs. Bippus, Pueblo, *The Mesa Workers' Cook Book,* 1897

Pork Cake

1 pound pork chopped fine, pour over this 1 pint boiling water, ½ pound figs, 1 pound raisins, ¼ pound citron, 1 pound currants, 2 cups dark sugar, 1 cup baking molasses, 1 pound English walnuts. Mix together flour enough to make stiff, 1 tablespoonful soda dissolved in a little hot water.

—Mrs. E. H. Price, Denver, *The Philalethean Cook Book,* 1911

Sunshine Cake

6 eggs, 1 cup granulated sugar, 1 cup flour, scant ⅓ teaspoonful cream tartar, pinch of salt, flavor to taste; sift, measure, and set aside flour and sugar; separate the eggs and add to the whites 1 pinch of salt; whip to a foam; add the cream tartar and whip until very stiff; add sugar and beat in; then add the well-beaten yolks; flavor and beat again; lastly, add the flour and fold lightly through; put in moderate oven at once and bake from 25 to 30 minutes.

—Columbine Sunshine Society, *How We Cook in Colorado,* 1907

Apple Snow

Pare, quarter, and bake 3 large apples. When cold, beat them with the white of 1 egg and 1 cup of pulverized sugar for a half hour. Make a boiled custard of 1 pint of milk, 2 eggs, and 2 tablespoonsful of sugar, flavor to taste. In serving put a tablespoonful of the snow in the center of each sauce dish and put the custard all around it.

—Marian Emmons, Denver, *How We Cook in Colorado*, 1907

Cheap Cake (no eggs, no butter, nor milk)

1 heaping tablespoonful lard; pour over this 1 cup strong coffee, then add 2 cups of brown sugar, 1 teaspoonful soda dissolved in a little hot water, 3 cups of flour sifted with ½ teaspoonful cloves and nutmeg, 1 teaspoonful cinnamon. This is good served warm with a good sauce.

—Mrs. W. A. Schliff, Gypsum, *Western Slope Cook Book*, 1912

My Mother's Ginger Snaps

1 cup New Orleans molasses, 2 tablespoonsful brown sugar, 3 table-spoonsful butter. Let all this come to boiling heat, then remove, and when cool, add 1 teaspoonful of soda, ginger, and flour enough to roll very thin.

—Mrs. T. B. Ives, Denver, *How We Cook in Colorado*, 1907

Suet Pudding

1 cup each molasses, sweet milk, suet (chopped fine), raisins, ½ cup currants, 2 ½ cups flour, ½ teaspoonful soda. Mix well. Spice and salt to taste. Steam 2 hours.

—Miss Dora Lindsey, Colorado Springs, *Good Housekeeping in High Altitudes*, 1888

Fig Pudding (very nice)

½ pound figs, chopped fine; ½ pound bread crumbs; 2 tablespoonsful flour; 1 cup brown sugar or molasses; 2 eggs; 1 cup suet, chopped fine; ½ of a grated nutmeg; 1 teaspoonful cinnamon. One cup candied lemon peel or citron can be added, as it is a great improvement. Rub the figs and sugar to a paste; mix with the bread crumbs and flour, and spice; beat the eggs very light and add them together with ½ teacup of milk, less milk if you use molasses. Put the mixture in a buttered mold and tie a thick floured cloth over it, and boil 4 hours steadily. Serve with sauce—egg, butter, or cream—a hard sauce.

—Mrs. G. Lamping, Denver,
The Twenty-Third Avenue Presbyterian Cook Book, 1897

Moonshine

Beat the whites of 6 eggs to a stiff froth, add slowly 6 tablespoonsful powdered sugar, beating for ½ hour; beat in 1 heaping tablespoonful of preserved peaches cut into small bits; set on ice until thoroughly cold. In serving, pour in each saucer some cream flavored with vanilla and sweetened, and on the cream place a portion of the moonshine.

—Mrs. A. T. King, Pueblo, *The Mesa Workers' Cook Book,* 1897

Grandmother's Sugar Cookies

2 eggs, 2 cups sugar, 1 cup butter, 1 cup sour milk, 2 teaspoonsful soda, 1 teaspoonful baking powder, 4 cups flour, over one-half nutmeg, 1 teaspoonful vanilla. Roll and sprinkle top of dough with sugar and cinnamon mixed. Bake in moderately hot oven.

—Mrs. Cynthia Wynne (born June 1, 1831), Colorado Springs,
Recipes of the First Congregational Church, 1920

Hermits

2 cups sugar, 1 cup butter, 1 cup raisins stoned and chopped, 3 eggs, 1 teaspoonful each cloves and cassia, nutmeg, ½ teaspoonful soda dissolved in 3 tablespoonsful of sweet milk, flour. Roll ¼ inch thick, cut round, and bake in a quick oven.

—*How We Cook in Colorado,* 1907

Delicious Desserts for Summer and Autumn Dinners

Summer

SUNDAY
Fruit Cream
Angel's Food
Roman Punch
Almond Drops

MONDAY
Cherry Pie

TUESDAY
Peach Cottage Pudding
Hard Sauce

WEDNESDAY
Strawberry Shortcake

THURSDAY
Strawberry Sherbet
White Pound Cake

FRIDAY
Charlotte Russe
Ring Jumbles

SATURDAY
Peach Pie

Autumn

SUNDAY
Peach Ice Cream
Caramel Cake

MONDAY
Railroad Pudding
Foaming Sauce

TUESDAY
Custard Pie

WEDNESDAY
Velvet Blanc Mange
Sugar Cookies

THURSDAY
Pumpkin Pie

FRIDAY
Coconut Pie

SATURDAY
Apple Fritters
White Wine Sauce

—Dr. Price's Delicious Desserts, 1904

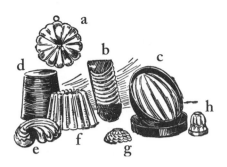

a. round fluted mold;
b. French bread pan;
c. melon mold;
d. pudding mold;
e. shell mold for jelly;
f. deep fluted mold;
g. individual shell mold for jelly or cream;
h. individual jelly mold

Plum Pudding to Englishmen's Taste, in Rhyme

To make plum-pudding to Englishmen's taste,
So all may be eaten and nothing to waste,
Take of raisins, and currants, and bread-crumbs, all round;
Also suet from oxen, and flour a pound,
Of citron well candied, or lemon as good,
With molasses and sugar, eight ounces, I would,
Into this first compound, next must be hasted
A nutmeg well grated, ground ginger well tasted,
With salt to preserve it, of such a teaspoonful;
Then of milk half a pint, and of fresh eggs take six;
Be sure after this that you properly mix.
Next tie up in a bag, just as round as you can,
Put into a capacious and suitable pan,
Then boil for eight hours just as hard as you can.

—*Dr. Chase's Third Last and Complete Receipt*
Book and Household Physician, 1903

BEVERAGES

Refreshing Summer Drinks
from Pueblo's Mesa Presbyterian Church

Mrs. John D. Kellogg's Spearmint Lemonade

Make a good lemonade and add to it a handful of bruised spearmint leaves. The mint will give it an agreeable flavor and fragrance.

Mrs. W. L. Graham's Nectar

6 lemons; 3 oranges; squeeze the juice out, and soak the rinds in water for an hour; squeeze these out and strain entire mixture. Sweeten to taste, and add water as for lemonade. Canned cherries and the juice give a delicious flavor, or when ripe red raspberries or strawberries can be obtained add either. When using the strawberries slice them, or one can use a part of a banana, slicing it very thin.

Mrs. Graham's Vendome

Prepare grapes as for jelly by washing and picking off stems; cook thoroughly in nearly as much water as grapes. Drain in jelly bag. I always squeeze some juice out, as not all the good rich juice drains through; sweeten to taste and boil until like wine or thicker; can air tight.

—*The Mesa Workers' Cook Book*, 1897

Bottling Spruce

Spruce Beer

Cold water, 10 gallons; boiling water, 11 gallons. Mix in a barrel, and add molasses, 30 pounds, or brown sugar, 24 pounds; essence of spruce, 1 ounce or more. Add 1 pint of yeast and ferment; bottle in 2 or 3 days. If you wish white spruce beer, use lump sugar.

Spruce Beer Powders

White sugar, 1 dram; bicarbonate of soda, 1 scruple; essence of spruce, 8 grains; essence of lemon, 1 grain. Mix and wrap it in blue paper. Then add tartaric acid, ½ dram, and wrap it in white paper. For use; dissolve each paper in separate glasses, one-third full of water, pour one into the other, and drink immediately.

Spruce Wine

Honey and sugar, each 50 pounds; soft water, 25 gallons; starch, made into jelly, 2 pounds; essence of spruce and cream of tartar, each ½ pound. Boil, then add essence of lemon, ¼ ounce; yeast, ½ pound. Bung close.

—Wright's book of 3000 practical receipts, 1869

Breakfast Coffee

This is to be mixed the night before. Mix 6 tablespoonful of coffee with the white of an egg (or smaller quantity if you like). Put into a small covered earthen dish, pour over it 2 cups of cold water, cover tightly, a preserve jar would do, and the next morning put into the coffee pot, pour the boiling water over it, using a cup to every tablespoonful, let it boil up just once, pour into it ½ cup of cold water, let settle a few minutes before serving. This can be made for after-dinner coffee by preparing in the morning.

—Mrs. T. L. Watson,
*The Rocky Mountain Cookbook for
High Altitude Cooking,* 1903

Raspberry Vinegar

Pour 1 quart of vinegar over 3 quarts of ripe black raspberries in a china vessel. Let it stand 24 hours, then strain it. Pour the liquor over 3 quarts of fresh raspberries and let it infuse again for a day and night; strain again and add 1 pound of white sugar to each pint of juice. Boil 20 minutes, skimming it well. Bottle when cold. When it is to be drunk, add 1 part of the raspberry vinegar to 4 parts of ice water.

—Nellie Walworth, Denver,
Our Kitchen Friend, 1899

The French coffee is reputed the best in the world, and a thousand voices have asked, What is it about the French coffee? In the first place, then, the French coffee is coffee, and not chicory, or rye, or beans, or peas. In the second place, it is freshly roasted, whenever made—roasted with great care and evenness in a little revolving cylinder which makes part of the furniture of every kitchen, and which keeps in the aroma of the berry. It is never overdone, so as to destroy the coffee flavor, which is in nine cases out of ten the fault of the coffee we meet with. Then it is ground, and placed in a coffeepot with a filter, through which it percolates in clear drops, the coffeepot standing on a heated stove to maintain the temperature. The nose of the coffeepot is stopped up to prevent the escape of the aroma during this process. The extract thus obtained is a perfectly clear, dark fluid, known as café noir, or black coffee. It is black only because of its strength, being in fact almost the very essential oil of coffee.

—Harriet Beecher Stowe,
House and Home Papers, 1869

Flax Seed Tea

Upon 1 ounce of whole flax-seed pour 1 pint of boiling water; place the vessel where it will keep warm for several hours; strain through fine cloth, add juice of 1 lemon, sweeten to taste.

—How We Cook in Colorado, 1907

Cider

To improve cider and keep it set, let the new cider from sour apples (sound and selected fruit is to be preferred), ferment from one to three weeks, as the weather is warm or cool. When it has attained to lively fermentation, add to each gallon, according to its acidity, from ½ to 2 pounds of white crushed sugar, and let the whole ferment until it possesses precisely the taste which it is desired should be permanent. In this condition, pour out a quart of the cider, and add for each gallon one quart of an ounce of sulphite of lime, known as an article of manufacture under the name of "anti-choloride of lime." Stir the powder and cider until intimately mixed and return the emulsion to the fermenting liquid. Agitate briskly and thoroughly for a few moments, and then let the cider settle. The fermentation will cease at once. When, after a few days, the cider has become clear, draw off and bottle carefully, or remove the sediment and return to the original vessel. If loosely corked, or kept in a barrel on draft, it will retain its taste as a still cider. If preserved in bottles carefully corked, which is better, it will become a sparkling cider, and may be kept indefinitely long.

—Durley Family Papers, 186?

Blackberry Cordial

2 quarts of ripe blackberries, 1 pound of loaf sugar, ½ ounce of cinnamon, ½ ounce of nutmegs, the same quantity of cloves and allspice. Boil together for a short time; when cold add 1 pint of brandy

—Mrs. Burnham, Denver, Our Kitchen Friend, 1899

Buttermilk

Farmers' families seldom appreciate what a delicious and healthful drink they have in homemade buttermilk. It was the fashionable drink in New York last summer, and brokers, bankers, and merchants indulged in it at three cents a glass, from street stands or wagons. Ice is not an essential where a beverage can be stood to cool in a porous earthen jar in a cold cellar or milk room, such as belongs to every farmhouse.

—*Healy & Bigelow's New Cook Book,* 1890

Chapter Fifteen

Company Expected: Recipes for Special Gatherings

TEAS & LUNCHEONS

For an afternoon out-of-door tea ... a pretty way to serve sandwiches is to roll them and tie them with different colored ribbons; a stoned olive can be put inside each one. Strawberries and cream, fancy cakes, Newport whips, iced tea, and seltzer lemonade will be sufficient for refreshments.

Austrian Coffee for Teas and Receptions

A coffee of the above name, sometimes served at teas and receptions, is a cold, strong coffee, creamed and sweetened. It is served in small glasses, with a tablespoon of ice cream added in each glass after the coffee is put in.

—*Mrs. Seely's Cook Book, 1902*

As we look to France for the best coffee, so we must look to England for the perfection of tea. The tea kettle is as much an English institution as aristocracy or the Prayer-Book; and when one wants to know exactly how tea should be made, one has only to ask how a fine old English housekeeper makes it. The first article of her faith is that the water must not merely be hot, not merely have boiled a few moments since, but be actually boiling at the moment it touches the tea. Hence, though servants in England are vastly better trained than with us, this delicate mystery is seldom left to their hands. Tea-making belongs to the drawing room, and high-born ladies preside at "the bubbling and loud-hissing urn," and see that all due rites and solemnities are properly performed—that the cups are hot, and that the infused tea waits the exact time before the libations commence.

—Harriet Beecher Stowe, *House and Home Papers,* 1869

Entrees from the Ladies of Denver's Twenty-Third Avenue Presbyterian Church

Mrs. McKean's Pressed Beef and Pork

Cook till very tender equal quantities of beef and pork; chop fine; season with pepper and salt, adding sage if desired; pack in square tin.

Mrs. Farmer's Oyster Rarebit

1 cup oysters; 2 tablespoonsful butter; ½ pound grated cheese; ¼ teaspoonful salt; a few grains cayenne; 2 eggs; 6 slices toast. Parboil the oysters and remove the tough muscle; drain and reserve the liquor; melt the butter, add the cheese and seasonings; beat the eggs and oyster liquor and add to the melted cheese; put in oysters and serve on toast.

—*The Twenty-Third Avenue Presbyterian Cook Book,* 1897

Sandwiches
from the Ladies of
Pueblo's Mesa Presbyterian Church

Egg and Onion Sandwiches

Boil eggs until hard; chop and mix with finely minced onion enough to taste, salt and mix with salad dressing and spread between buttered bread.

Lettuce and Nut Sandwiches

Cut bread very thin; trim off crusts, then butter; place lettuce leaves between and spread with mayonnaise dressing mixed with whipped cream and any kind of nuts chopped and mixed with dressing.

Tongue Sandwiches

Slice thin smoked tongue; place between pieces of buttered rye or white bread; add mustard if desired.

—*The Mesa Workers' Cook Book,* 1897

Afternoon Teas

A new wrinkle at afternoon teas is the service of crackers or wafers spread with Sunkist Orange. Put together sandwich fashion and heat in the oven just long enough to allow the flavor and juice of the fruit to penetrate the cracker and soften it slightly.

—*Recipes for Dainty Dishes,*
ca. 1910s

Colorado Springs, November 2, 1871

Drove up to Glen Eyrie for tea. Glen Eyrie lies about five miles north-west of town, between the Garden of the Gods and Monument Park. It is a valley in the foothills, about half a mile long and a little less broad, shut in from the plains by a rock wall, which runs almost from Cheyenne Mountain to Monument Park, some fourteen miles, varying in height from fifty feet to some hundred, with here and there a gateway through to some valley or canyon. The P.s are building a most charming large house; but till it is finished they live in a sort of picnic way, in rooms 10 x 10, partitioned off from the loft over the stable! Their servant had cooked some excellent venison and "flapjacks" for us; and we had Californian honey, blackberry preserve, first-rate coffee, and baked potatoes

Colorado Springs, November 7, 1871

We invited Dr. B. and Mr. __ to tea in honour of my birthday, and M. and I had great fun preparing for our house-warming. He went out and got a white teapot and milk-jug, six tin mugs, six forks, knives, tea-spoons, and plates; a tin basis for washing the dishes, a packet of tea and sugar, a bag of crackers (biscuits), and two boxes of sardines. We laid the table in English sytle and felt quite "high-toned"—to use a Westernism—when our guests came in. We thoroughly enjoyed being four Britishers together so far away from the old country; and, after our sumptuous tea, sat chatting and singing songs round the stove till eight, when our party dispersed, as the haunting demon of America—business—called for their services again, and M. got out his office book, and I answered home-letters.

—*South by West or Winter in the Rocky Mountains*, 1874

Ending on a Sweet Note

Lady's Cake

½ cup butter, 1 ½ cups sugar, 2 cups flour, 1 cup sweet milk, whites of 4 eggs, 1 teaspoonful cream tartar, ½ teaspoonful soda.

—Mrs. Pierson, Colorado Springs,
Good Housekeeping in High Altitudes, 1888

Fruit Cake

4 pounds of raisins, 2 of currants, 2 of figs, 1 of citron, 12 eggs, 1 pound white powdered sugar, 1 pint of syrup, 1 of brandy, 1 of wine, 1 table-spoonful of cloves, 1 of cinnamon, 3 nutmegs, 1 pound of flour, 1 of butter, 1 bottle (small) lemon essence, 5 teaspoonsful baking powder.

—Mrs. Clark, Denver,
Our Kitchen Friend, 1889

Tea Cake

1 cup sugar, 1 tablespoonful butter, 2 eggs well beaten, 1 cup sweet milk, 1 ½ teaspoonsful baking powder, 1 teaspoonful lemon or vanilla extract. Flour enough for pretty thick butter. Bake in hot gem pans.

—Miss F. L. Raymond, Leadville
Cloud City Cook-Book, 1889

Green Gooseberry Tart

Top and tail the gooseberries. Put into a porcelain kettle with enough water to prevent burning, and stew slowly until they break. Take them off, sweeten well, and set aside to cool. When cold, pour into pastry shells, and bake with a top crust of puff-paste. Brush with beaten egg while hot; set back in the oven to glaze for 3 minutes. Eat cold.

—*Common Sense in the Household*, 1871

Delicious Desserts for Spring Teas or Luncheons

SUNDAY	Lemon Jelly ✤ Gold Cake
MONDAY	Floating Island ✤ Chocolate Cake
TUESDAY	Sliced Oranges ✤ Philadelphia Jumbles
WEDNESDAY	Boston Cream Cakes
THURSDAY	Currant and Raspberry Tarts with whipped cream
FRIDAY	Cup Custard ✤ Fruit Cookies
SATURDAY	Baked Sweet Apples with whipped cream Clove Cake

—Dr. Price's Delicious Desserts, 1904

What Will You Have?

Thank you—a plate of any thing. Have you been to a country tea-party before?

No, never; I like it. Why do so many keep utter silence, though? A good many have only opened their mouths to eat, not to speak.

It is our way. Tomorrow they will speak fast enough; we shall be turned into hash.

Yet you invite such?

Oh, we must invite each other; we live so. Our events often come from these insignificant meetings.

Does that elderly young lady enjoy herself, for instance? And he pointed to a silent spinster who held her third teacup, and who was looking everywhere with wide eyes.

Certainly. She has the pattern of all our dresses in her head, and can set forth our manners, and repeat all that has been said, at any moment from this table.

The bashful young man, who laughs so much, is he really entertained?

He is bashful here; but tomorrow, in the shops or loafing-places, he will be very bold and sneering in his remarks upon my attempt at society.

I see, a tea-party is like others; or human nature in general.

—"The Tea-Party," in *Appletons' Journal,* October 1871

☞ *Sandwich Fillings for Picnics* ☜
and Daytime Gatherings

☞ *Vegetable*: 1 ounce rhubarb juice, 1 ounce peanuts, 1 ounce carrots, and 1 ounce celery.

☞ Cottage cheese and chopped dates.

☞ Grated cheese and minced onion.

☞ Lettuce, cream cheese, and chopped olives.

☞ Equal parts dates, peanut butter, and cream cheese.

☞ Crisp cucumber, dry and dip in dressing and place between binders.

☞ Peel and grate 1 tart apple; mix ½ cup cream cheese and 1 tablespoonful cream. Add apple and mix.

☞ Flaked peanuts moistened with lemon juice and honey.

☞ Lettuce and peanut butter mixed with lemon juice. Put peanut butter mixture on buttered bread and lay on lettuce leaves.

—*International Health Resort Recipes,* 1900

RECIPES FOR OTHER OCCASIONS

VALENTINE'S DAY

Honor Sandwiches for St. Valentine's Tea

Cut white bread in ¼-inch slices and shape with heart cutter. Spread with pimento butter, put together in pairs, and arrange on a fancy plate covered with a doily.

Pimento butter—Cream 2 tablespoonsful butter, add 1 canned pimento forced through a sieve, and work until thoroughly blended; then season with salt.

—*Catering for Special Occasions,* 1911

FOURTH OF JULY

Fourth of July Punch

1 cup sugar, ½ cup water, 1 can sliced pineapple cut in pieces, 2 lemons, 2 oranges, ½ cup raspberry syrup, ¼ cup brandy, 1 pint bottle Moselle wine, 1 pint bottle Apollinaris. Boil sugar and water 5 minutes; add juice from lemons and oranges as well as remaining ingredients. Pour over a cake of ice.

—*Catering for Special Occasions,* 1911

THANKSGIVING

Pumpkin Pie (fine)

1 quart stewed mashed pumpkin, 1 pint rich milk, 3 eggs beaten together, ¾ cup light brown sugar (granulated will answer), ½ tablespoonful cinnamon, ½ teaspoonful each of allspice, salt, ginger, ¼ nutmeg grated, juice of ½ lemon. Mix all ingredients together thoroughly, pour into two crusts, and bake about ½ hour in moderate oven.

—Virginia M. Shafroth (Mrs. John F.), wife of Colorado Governor, *Round Table Cook Book,* 1910

Mince Meat Pie

4 pounds of apples, 3 of currants, 2 of raisins, 2 of citron, 2 of almonds, 3 of butter, and 2 quarts of brandy. Peel and chop fine the apples, wash and dry the currants, stone the raisins, cut fine the citron and blanche the almonds. Mix all the ingredients together, add mace, cinnamon, cloves, nutmeg, allspice, and sugar to taste. When ready to bake, add more brandy, sugar, and butter.

—Mrs. Cronkhite, Denver, *Our Kitchen Friend,* 1889

Roast Goose

Stuff the goose with potato dressing. Truss and dredge well with salt, pepper, and flour. Roast (if 8 pounds) 1 ¼ hour. No butter is required for goose, since it is so fat. Serve with applesauce.

Potato Dressing:

6 potatoes, 1 tablespoonful salt, 1 tablespoonful pepper, 1 teaspoonful sage, 2 tablespoonsful onion juice, 2 tablespoonsful butter. Boil potatoes; pare them, then mash them fine and light. Combine all.

—*Sloan's Cook Book and Advice to Housekeepers,* 1905

November 8, 1866

I have baked five pumkin pies today. They are the first ones I have made since I left Boonville (N.Y.). It had been three months & I had allmost forgoten how. The milk was given to us by Mrs. Ranger Jones.

—Amelia Butts (Mrs. George) Buss, *Diary,* 1866-1867

Thanksgiving Dinner

For the table I prefer a white cloth with fancy border and napkins to match. A dash of color livens up the table in the bleak November when flowers cannot be had in profusion. Casters in the center, of course, flanked by tall celery glasses. At each end, glass fruit dishes filled with apples and nuts. A bottle of pepper sauce near the casters, a mold of jelly by the platter of turkey, and small side dishes of chopped cabbage garnished with rings of cold boiled eggs. The purple cabbage makes the handsomest-looking dishes. Serve the soup from tureens into soup dishes, handing around to the guests. After this comes the piece de resistance, "Thanksgiving turkey." A piece of dark meat with a spoonful of gravy, and one of white with a bit of jelly and a baked potato (I should prefer a spoonful of mashed) should be served on each plate, leaving the other vegetables to be passed afterward with the roast pig. After this the salad, and then the plates should be taken away and the dessert served. Then come the apples and nuts, the tea and coffee, well seasoned with grandpa's old-time stories, grandma's quaint sayings, and kind words and merry repartees from all.

—Dr. Chase's Third Last and Complete
Receipt Book and Household Physician, 1903

CHRISTMAS

To Prepare a Turkey for Christmas Dinner

The turkey should be cooped up and fed some time before Christmas. Three days before it is slaughtered, it should have an English walnut forced down its throat three times a day, and a glass of sherry once a day. The meat will be deliciously tender and have a fine nutty flavor.

—Statesmen's Dishes and How to Cook Them, 1890

Spice Bread

This makes 11 loaves and is very good for the holidays; will keep a long time. Sift flour enough for 8 loaves of white bread. Add 2 pounds of lard, 3 pints of sugar, 2 pounds of currants, ¼ pound of raisins, 1 pound of citron, 2 tablespoonsful of salt, 1 teaspoonful of cinnamon, allspice, cloves, mace, and nutmeg. Brown 1 cup of sugar on the stove and add a little water; make your sponge as you would for light bread. Make it an noon, let is rise till evening, then pat your flour in your brad pan and add sponge and all the rest; mix not very stiff. In morning make in loaves, bake in slow oven 1 ½ hours.

*—Mrs. Barthell, Gypsum, *Western Slope Cook Book*, 1912*

Christmas Plum Pudding

Chop and rub to a cream ¼ pound of suet, add scant ½ pound sugar; mix well. Add 4 well-beaten eggs, 1 grated nutmeg, ½ teaspoonful each cloves, mace, and salt, ½ cup brandy, ¾ cup milk, flour to make a thin batter. Seed and shop ½ pound raisins, wash clean ½ pound currants, cut into thin slices ½ pound citron. Sprinkle fruits with flour to prevent their settling to the bottom of batter. Steam 5 to 8 hours.

SAUCE FOR PUDDING: Cream 2 cups of butter, add slowly 1 cup powdered sugar, the unbeaten white of 1 egg, 2 tablespoonsful of wine and 1 of brandy, ¼ cup boiling water. Heat until smooth and creamy. Heat the bowl for the creamed butter, and when adding wine do so slowly to prevent curdling. This pudding will keep for a year. As it can be prepared beforehand, it is excellent for Christmas, saving much labor on that busy day.

—Mrs. H. C. Dimick, Leadville, *Cloud City Cook-Book,* 1899

Menu for Christmas Dinner

Consommé   Bread Sticks

Olives   Celery   Salted Pecans

Roast Goose   Potato Stuffing   Apple Sauce

Duchess Potatoes   Cream of Lima Beans

Chicken Croquettes with Green Peas

Dressed Lettuce with Cheese Straws

English Plum Pudding   Brandy Sauce

Frozen Pudding   Assorted Cake   Bonbons

Crackers   Cheese   Café Noir

—*The Boston Cooking-School Cook Book,* 1896

Twelfth Night Cake

Beat to a cream 1 cupful of butter and 2 of granulated sugar. Beat the whites and yolks of 6 eggs separately; beat the yolks into the creamed butter and sugar, a little at a time, then add ½ cup of milk alternately with 3 cups of flour that has 1 teaspoonful of baking powder sifted with it, then fold in the beaten whites of the eggs, lastly add the grated rind and juice of ½ lemon, a cup of seeded raisins soaked in brandy and rolled in flour, and a teaspoonful of caraway seeds. Bake in a round pan with a tube in the center, line it with buttered paper. Roll the silver pieces in thin white paper, then in flour; place in opposite sides of the cake. Bake slowly. When cold, ice with a thick white frosting, decorate with candied cherries and angelica, surround with holly, and stick a piece in the center.

—The Rocky Mountain Cookbook for High Altitude Cooking, 1903

Eve's Pudding

If you want a good pudding, mind what you are taught;
Take eggs, six in number, when bought for a groat,
The fruit with which Eve her husband did cozen,
Well pared, and well chopped, at least half a dozen;
Six ounces of bread, let Moll eat the crust,
And crumble the rest as fine as the dust;
Six ounces of currants, from the stem you must sort,
Lest you break out your teeth, and spoil all the sport;
Six ounces of sugar won't make it too sweet,
Some salt and some nugmeg will make it complete;
Three hours let it boil without any flutter.
But Adam won't like it without wine and butter..

—Custer County Women's Club

WEDDINGS

Wedding Cake

50 eggs, 5 pounds sugar, 5 pounds flour, 5 pounds butter, 15 pounds raisins, 3 pounds citron, 10 pounds currants, 1 pint brandy, ¼ ounce cloves, 1 ounce cinnamon, 4 ounces mace, 4 ounces nutmeg. This makes 43 ½ pounds and keeps 20 years.

—*Centennial Buckeye Cookbook,* 1876

Bride's Cake

¾ pound butter; 1 pound flour; 1 pound pulverized sugar; 18 eggs (whites of); 1 pound blanched almonds rolled very fine; flavor with extract of peach; 3 teaspoonsful baking powder (if desired). To blanch almonds immerse them in hot water and strip them of their skins.

—Mrs. Dimock, Denver,
The Twenty-Third Avenue Presbyterian Cook Book, 1897

BIRTHDAYS

Birthday Cake

1 cup butter, 2 cups sugar, 3 cups flour, 4 eggs, 3 teaspoonsful baking powder. Mix with milk and flavor.

—Miss Ellen Stephens, Colorado Springs,
Good Housekeeping in High Altitudes, 1888

CHAPTER SIXTEEN

$\mathcal{F}$OR THE LADY AS HOSTESS

Receiving Your Husband's Guests

Especially, let your welcome be ready and hearty when your husband brings home an unexpected guest.

UNDERSTAND HIM. Take care he understands clearly that this is his prerogative and that the rules by which you would govern the visits of your own sex are not applicable to his. Men rarely set seasons for their visits. They snatch an hour or two with an old chum or new friend out of the hurry of business life, as one stoops to pluck a stray violet from a dusty roadside. Your husband must take his chances when he can get them.

WELCOME HIS GUESTS GLADLY. If he can walk home, arm in arm, with the school fellow he has not seen in ten years, not only fearlessly, but gladly anticipatory of your pleasure at the sight of him; if, when the stranger is presented to you, you receive him as your friend because he is your husband's and seat him to a family dinner, plain, but nicely served, and eaten in cheerfulness of heart; if the children are well behaved and your attire that of a lady who has not lost the desire to look her best in her husband's eyes, then you have added to the links of steel that knit your husband's heart to yours.

My wife, I will not deny, was a little elated at the idea of having a city Editor to dinner; but when I repeated, one by one, your extraordinary expectations, she became very thoughtful and silent. Why you see, sir, the "spring chickens" we could count upon, by-and-bye; but the "trout," the "woodcock," the "snipe," the "wild ducks," and, coolest of propositions, that all these should be brought on consecutively, keeping half a dozen cooks busy, and quite confounding my father and my dear old aunt with such unheard-of proceedings—all these, and ices and wines, in our quiet country home—Oh, sir, I blush at the thought of it. Moreover, I withdraw the invitation. Don't come to dinner. I forbid it.

—*Country Margins and Rambles of a Journalist*, 1855

Guests in Your Home

REQUEST NOTIFICATION OF A VISIT. Do not be ashamed to say to your nearest of kin or the confidante of your school days, "Always let me know when to look for you." If you are the woman I take you to be—methodical, industrious, and ruling your household according to just and firm laws of order and punctuality—you need this notice.

UPON INVITATION, STATE THE LENGTH OF THE VISIT. Mention the day when you would be happy to receive them and the length of time of their visit. Perhaps a young lady is invited to make a visit in the country, or in the city, and no mention is made of days, weeks, or months, for its limit; therefore, she is utterly at a loss to know what amount of clothing, etc., she may require.

WELCOME THEM SIMPLY. Welcome the coming guest with a few, simple, pleasant, easy words and without ostentatious cordiality; without gushing declarations of friendship; without paralyzing his arm by an interminable shaking of hands; without hurry, flourish, and due anxiety to have his trunk carried up to his room; or sandwiching between every sentence an anxious appeal to make himself entirely at home—an appeal which usually operates to make one feel as much away from home as possible.

ENABLE HIM TO HELP HIMSELF. The art of hospitality consists in making the guest forget that he is a guest and in leaving to him the exercise of his senses and of responsibility, at least so far that, finding what he needs at his hand, he may help himself.

HAVE THE FIRE READY. It is merciless to invite friends to visit you in cold weather without providing a fire in their bedroom or dressing room. Neither is it courteous to wait until they arrive, and then inquire, "Would you like a fire?" Therefore, if you cannot afford to make your friends comfortable, do not invite them; at least in the wintry season.

A HOME PREPARED FOR A GUEST LOOKS THUS:

- The additional place is set at the table.
- Your spare bed, which yesterday was tossed into a heap, has both mattresses aired, is covered lightly with a thin spread, and is made up with fresh sheets that have not gathered damp.
- The room is bright and dustless.
- Towels are aplenty, fresh soap is in the dish, fresh ink in the inkstand, fresh pen in the holder, stationery at hand, and the pin cushion well supplied with pins.
- Candles, matches, and water are on the stand by the bedside.
- The drawers of closet and bureau are empty and, if sachets are not supplied, smooth white paper is spread in them.
- The dainty dish is prepared for dinner or tea so as to be off your mind.

- ✦ Your husband knows whom he is to see at his homecoming.
- ✦ The children are clean and on the qui vive—children's instincts are always hospitable.
- ✦ The guest's welcome is given in the air of such a house. Perhaps, as she lays aside her traveling dress, she smiles at your "ceremonious, old-maidish ways" and marvels that so good a manager should deem such forms necessary with an old friend.

RECEIVE UNANNOUNCED VISITORS HAPPILY. Since unlooked-for visitors will occasionally drop in upon the best-regulated families, make it your study to receive them gracefully and cordially. If they care enough for you to turn aside from their regular route to tarry a day, night, or week with you, it would be churlish not to show appreciation of the favor in which you are held. Make them welcome to the best you can offer at so short notice, and let no preoccupied air or troubled smile be token to your perturbation.

PUT UP LUNCHEON UPON THEIR DEPARTURE. It is a graceful act to provide a pasteboard box of lunch for a departing visitor, as during a long journey the opportunities for a comfortable meal are often lacking. Most ladies, myself among the number, would usually prefer to go without a dinner than to hurry to the counter of a railway dining saloon, give an order, and attempt to eat and drink with one eye on the clock and the other on the cars.

☞ *Chicken Lunch for Traveling*

Cut a young chicken down the back; wash and wipe dry; season with salt and pepper; put in a dripping pan and bake in a moderate oven three-quarters of an hour. This is much better for traveling lunch than when seasoned with butter.

—*The White House Cook Book,* 1887

CHAPTER SEVENTEEN

$\mathcal{F}$OR THE LADY VISITOR, THE LADY CALLER, AND THE LADY CORRESPONDENT

The Visitor

There is the art, too, of making oneself agreeable as a guest.

NOTIFY YOUR HOSTESS IN ADVANCE. Laying to your conduct the line and plummet of the Golden Rule, never pay a visit (I use the word in contra-distinction to "call") without notifying your hostess-elect of your intention thus to favor her. Perhaps once in ten thousand times, your friend—be she mother, sister, or intimate acquaintance—may be enraptured at your unexpected appearance, traveling satchel in hand, at her door to pass a day, a night, or a month. But the chances are so greatly in favor of the probability that you will upset her household arrangements, abrade her temper, or put her to undue trouble or embarrassment, that it is hardly worth your while to risk so much in order to gain so little.

ADAPT YOURSELF. Endeavor to conform, without apparent effort, to the arrangements of the family with whom you board and to the manners and customs of the people around you, as far as they do not compromise your principles of good morals and good taste. If you don't like a thing, let it alone; eat nothing, and by the next meal you may be glad to eat anything.

TAKE CONGENIALITY. Be cheerful, be kind, be considerate, be accommodating. Shun argument and controversy on any and all subjects. Do not obtrude your political or religious sentiments. Let your courtesy come out naturally, and if religious, don't be a Pharisee.

AVOID DINING RUDENESS. Blowing soup or pouring tea and coffee into the saucer to cool is evidence of a lack of knowledge of the usage of good society. Beware, lest you make that disagreeable sound in eating soup which is not only offensive to the ear but is a positive rudeness. Do not eat all on your plate and do not clean it up with your bread. In a dinner of several courses, it is unusual for a guest to ask for any dish a second time.

> The Christmas-eve closed in dark and misty before our travelers at last arrived. They had been delayed on the mountains by a thick falling mist which obliged them to great caution, for shelving rocks and deep gorges bordered the winding road. Mounted men with torches, and giving cheery hails, had gone far to meet them, and once down into our valley the blaze of lights from our broad Queen Anne windows made a welcoming beacon. It was a home-coming of delighted surprises—what a happy clamor it was! And my "surprise" was approved and praised to my heart's content. My New York friend had no words to express her astonishment and delight—the open piano caught her eye and straightway her splendid voice filled my hungry ears with triumphant song. But hungry people claimed her for supper: "Bouillon, mayonnaise! game pate! jellies, wedding-cakes, and all Delmonico's!" The two days travel across solitary plains with frontier stopping-places closing with the risky mountain crossing in the dark made it, as she said, "a transformation-scene" to come out of the night and the mist into this vision of a New York home—enriched by a frontier welcome.
>
> —Jessie Benton Freemont, *Far-West Sketches*, 1890

RECIPROCATE YOUR HOST'S WELCOME. A dinner invitation should always be returned during the social season; that is, before people separate for the summer. If the recipient has not an establishment which admits of giving a dinner in return, a ride or drive in the country, a good restaurant dinner, or a theatre party in the city is considered a social equivalent.

☞ Hints for Plains Travelers ☜

❋ The best seat inside a stagecoach is the one next to the driver ... you will get less than half the bumps and jars than on any other seat. When any old "sly Eph," who traveled thousands of miles on coaches, offers through sympathy to exchange his back or middle seat with you, don't do it.

❋ Never ride in cold weather with tight boots or shoes, nor close-fitting gloves. Bathe your feet before starting in cold water, and wear loose overshoes and gloves two or three sizes too large.

❋ When the driver asks you to get off and walk, do it without grumbling. He will not request it unless absolutely necessary. If a team runs away, sit still and take your chances; if you jump, nine times out of ten you will be hurt.

❋ In very cold weather, abstain entirely from liquor while on the road; a man will freeze twice as quick while under its influence.

❋ Don't growl at food stations; stage companies generally provide the best they can get. Don't keep the stage waiting; many a virtuous man has lost his character by so doing.

❋ Don't smoke a strong pipe inside, especially early in the morning. Spit on the leeward side of the coach. If you have anything to take in a bottle, pass it around; a man who drinks by himself in such a case is lost to all human feeling. Provide stimulants before starting; ranch whisky is not always nectar.

⊛ Don't swear, nor lop over on your neighbor when sleeping. Don't ask how far it is to the next station.

⊛ Never attempt to fire a gun or pistol while on the road; it may frighten the team; and the careless handling and cocking of the weapon makes nervous people nervous.

⊛ Don't discuss politics or religion, nor point out places on the road where horrible murders have been committed.

⊛ Don't linger too long at the pewter wash basin at the station.

⊛ Don't grease your hair before starting or dust will stick there in sufficient quantities to make a respectable 'tater' patch. Tie a silk handkerchief around your neck to keep out dust and prevent sunburns.

⊛ Don't imagine for a moment you are going on a picnic; expect annoyance, discomfort, and some hardships. If you are disappointed, thank heaven.

—*The Omaha Herald,* 1877

RESPECT THEIR PRIVACY. The Arab never speaks ill of those whose salt he has tasted; and well-bred persons will never repeat what Mrs. A. said, nor tell what Mr. A. did, when they were visiting at their house.

REMEMBER THE SERVANTS. Visitors should always give the servants who have waited upon them some little presents, either in money or its equivalent. They have had extra work in waiting upon them and deserve extra compensation.

The Caller

Calls cement the acquaintance with all whom you admit to your circle.

REMEMBER THE IMPORTANCE OF CALLING. Formal calls in the city are intended to serve in lieu of the more genial and lengthy visits which are a part of country life. Calling is the surest way to maintain agreeable acquaintances and foster those friendships which brighten life.

Waiting for the mail-carriers to beat down the snow in their track, we remained a few days with the two brothers, and enjoyed the bounteous repasts and good cheer of the station, with its bachelor proprietors. The housekeeping and culinary duties were there attended to as well as if a woman had been at the helm; and all indoors breathed of home comfort, though the furniture was of the simplest and rudest kind, mostly made by their own hands. These gentlemen, with a greatness of heart that was characteristic of the Colorado man at that date, pressed us to remain with them until the snow should disappear. That might have meant a waiting until spring, and no doubt they would have accepted the joke good-naturedly, as they said our company was well worth our keeping; but as we learned they would accept no payment for their care of us, we moved on as soon as we could safely do so, and we took with us what the two brothers said we were leaving, as we parted company with them—a memory of a pleasant acquaintance.

—Dagmar Mariager, "Camp and Travel in Colorado,"
in *Overland Monthly and Out West Magazine*, January 1890

Acquaint Yourself with Appropriate Occasions for Calls:

❧ Visits of ceremony, are those which are paid after receiving attentions at the hands of your acquaintances; after dining or supping at a friend's house; after attending an evening party; etc.; and they should invariably be of short duration. One should never take either children or dogs when making them. Hand your card to the servant at the door, and ask if the lady or ladies are in. After attending a dinner party or a ball, you should call within the week upon your hostess.

❧ Formal visits are usually paid between the hours of noon and three o'clock; informal visits at those hours when you know your friends are at leisure to receive you. It is well, in making social visits, however, not to acquire the title of a day goblin—one who, having no occupation, and delighting in the sound of his or her own voice, makes constant inroads into their friends' houses and runs in at the most unseasonable hours, saying, "Oh! it is only I, nobody minds me; let me come right up stairs."

Visits of congratulation are paid after the birth of an infant, when it is also customary to send tasteful and elegant baskets or bouquets of flowers. Also, upon friends who have received an appointment to any office or dignity in the community, state, or government. If a friend has published a book, you call to congratulate him upon its success; or if he has delivered a lecture, sermon, or oration, which has elicited your applause, you call and express your high estimation of the discourse. And you pay visits of congratulation when you hear that your friends are intending to marry, and take upon themselves new responsibilities.

Several Callers at Once

If when making a social call a second visitor arrives, the first caller, if she has made a call of sufficient length, should after a few minutes take her leave. When calling, if a lady find several persons have preceded her, she should invariably greet the hostess first, ignoring all others until this courtesy is shown.

—*Sloan's Cook Book and Advice to Housekeepers*, 1905

In this world of sickness, sorrow, and bereavement, visits of condolence must occasionally be made; and, if possible, they should be paid within a week after death has entered the family circle. If your acquaintance is ceremonious, it is the custom, however, to wait until the family have appeared at church.

If you have a friend who has met reverses and you desire to show your friendship by visiting her, do not go dressed expensively. Adapt your dress to her changed circumstances.

REFRAIN FROM CALLING ONLY IF YOU ARE PREPARED TO QUIT THE FRIENDSHIP. If, previous to a long voyage, or absence, or on the occasion of your marriage, you omit to call or send a card to your friends, it is understood that the acquaintance ceases. When you return home, those to whom you have sent cards, or paid visits, will pay the first visit to you.

CALL AT THE PROPER TIMES. Morning calls, are not, as their title would imply, calls made in the forenoon but embrace the hours from one o' clock to five o' clock. They are generally of 15 or 20 minutes in duration. Calls in the evening are made from eight o' clock to nine o' clock and should be of an hour's duration. A gentleman whose time is his own can call between two o' clock and five o' clock. But, as business engrosses nearly all our gentlemen, from eight to half-past eight o' clock in the evening is the proper time to make a social call. If he calls before that hour, he may interfere with some previous engagement his hostess may have and will surely displease her by his eagerness. Dress suits are for evening calls.

DEPORT YOURSELF PROPERLY DURING CALLS:

* While waiting in the parlor for the lady on whom you call to appear, the piano must remain untouched, as also the bric-a-brac.

* Sit quietly in the place the servant has assigned you, and rise when the hostess enters. The outer wraps are retained while making calls, the brief time allowed for remaining making it unnecessary to remove them.

* In making a ceremonious call, a gentleman's hat and cane are retained in his hand and his gloves remain on, but an umbrella is left in the hall.

* Do not enter into grave discussions; trifling subjects are better.

* Do not draw near the fire when calling unless invited.

The Correspondent

KNOW THE PURPOSES AND ETI-
QUETTE FOR WRITING LET-
TERS OF DIFFERING TYPES:

◈ Letters of introduction are used to introduce one friend to another who lives at some distance. Do not give a letter of introduction to anyone with whom you are not thoroughly acquainted. Such letters are generally left unsealed, and the name of the person introduced should be written on the lower left-hand corner of the envelope, in order that the persons on meeting may greet each other without embarrassment.

Mrs. Sherwood & Jessie came here for a call this afternoon & staid two hours but did not take off their things. They came with a sleigh or rather a substitute for a sleigh.

—Amelia Butts (Mrs. George) Buss, *Diary*, 1866-1867

◈ Letters of friendship or letters among very intimate friends, admit of less formal terms, such as Very sincerely yours, Your dutiful son, Your affectionate nephew, etc. The chief essentials in letters of friendship are that the style be simple and the manner of expression be natural; it is the incidents of everyday life, the little things, the home chat that make a friendship letter interesting.

◈ Never write a letter when you are laboring under great excitement, for you will almost certainly write things that you will repent next day. When constrained to write severe things, the letter should be permitted to lie overnight for review before mailing. If this be done, it is probable that the character of the letter will be changed radically, or perhaps it will remain unwritten. Many letters which would seem ample provocation for a sharp reply had better go unanswered. Kind words make and hold friends, while hasty or vindictive words alienate friends.

◈ Letters of courtesy include invitations, acceptances, letters of congratulation, of condolence, of introduction, and of recommendation, all of which are more formal in style than letters of friendship.

To write a good love letter you ought to begin without knowing what you are going to say and finish without knowing what you have written.

REMEMBER THESE RULES WHEN WRITING A LETTER:

In writing a letter, place the date within an inch or two of the top, at the right-hand, and be sure to write the name of the town, county, and state, with the date of the month and year; if living in a city, give the street and number also.

No gentleman or lady ever writes an anonymous letter.

Do not fill your letters with apologies and mere repetitions.

Avoid writing with a pencil or with other than black or blue-black ink.

Letters about one's own affairs, requiring an answer, should always enclose a stamp, to pay return postage.

Short sentences are easier to write than long ones, hence more suitable for correspondence.

The signature should be written very plainly, for no matter how familiar your intimate friends are with your dashing ink lines, others may have considerable difficulty in associating them with your printed name.

In social correspondence, the envelopes, like the paper, should be white and plain, and should correspond to the paper used in size and quality. It is considered bad taste to use colored paper, or other than black ink.

Be sure to write to a friend, or hostess, after making a visit at her house, thanking her for her hospitality. Don't wait a fortnight before doing so.

It is the fault of the English language that we have so many "bad spellers." If you are doubtful of a word, it will be better to look it up rather than make a blot, or a running line, where the letters are questioned. Careful reading, and lots of it, will make a good speller.

Chapter Eighteen

For the Lady in Mourning

Mourning Practices

FOLLOW THESE GUIDELINES FOR MOURNING:

🕊 A widow's mourning should last 18 months. The color of black for heavy mourning should be a dull dead hue, not a blue-black nor yet with any brown shade. For the first six months, the dress should be of crape cloth or Henrietta cloth covered entirely with crape, collar and cuffs of white crape, a crape bonnet with a long crape veil, and a widow's cap of white crape if preferred. After six months' mourning, the crape can be removed and grenadine trimmings used, if the smell of crape is offensive, as it is to some people. After 12 months, the widow's cap is left off and the heavy veil is exchanged for a lighter one. The dress can be of silk grenadine, plain black gros grain, or crape-trimmed cashmere with jet trimmings, and crepe lisse about the neck and sleeves. Bows, flowers, and decorative finishing generally are wholly out of place in deep mourning; lace and embroidery are wholly inadmissible.

🕊 The veil is always of crape and in this country is worn very long—most inconveniently and absurdly so, indeed. This fashion is very much objected to by doctors, who think many diseases of the eye come by this means. The crape also sheds its pernicious dye into the sensitive nostrils, producing catarrhal disease as well as blindness and cataract of the eye. It is a thousand pities that fashion dictates the crape veil, but so it is. It is the very banner of woe, and no one has the courage to go without it. We can only suggest to mourners wearing it that they should pin a small veil of black tulle over the eyes and nose and throw back the heavy crape as often as possible, for health's sake.

❧ Mourning for a father or mother should last one year. A deep veil is worn at the back of the bonnet, but not over the head or face like the widow's veil, which covers the entire person when down. Mourning for a brother or sister, for stepfather or stepmother, and for grandparents may be the same as for the parents, but the duration may be shorter.

❧ The period of mourning for an aunt or uncle or cousin is of three months' duration.

❧ Wives and husbands wear mourning for relatives of their spouses.

❧ Mourning for children should last nine months. In the first three months, the dress should be crape-trimmed, the mourning less deep than that for a husband. No one is ever ready to take off mourning; therefore these rules have this advantage—they enable the friends around a grief-stricken mother to tell her when is the time to make her dress more cheerful, which she is bound to do for the sake of the survivors, many of whom are perhaps affected for life by seeing a mother always in black. It is well for mothers to remember this when sorrow for a lost child makes all the earth seem barren to them.

Funeral Etiquette

DRESS THE DECEASED SIMPLY. In dressing the remains for the grave, those of a man are usually "clad in his habit as he lived." For a woman, tastes differ; a white robe and cap, not necessarily shroud-like, are decidedly unexceptionable. For young persons and children, white cashmere robes and flowers are always most appropriate.

USE FLOWERS SPARINGLY. A few flowers placed in the dead hand—perhaps a simple wreath—is plenty, but not those unmeaning memorials which have become to real mourners such sad perversities of good taste and such a misuse of flowers. Let those who can afford to send such things devote the money to the use of poor mothers who cannot afford to buy a coffin for a dead child or a coat for a living one.

He took me to none of the costly monuments, nor graves of famous folk, but wandered here and there among the trees, his hands clasped behind him, stopping now and then at a green mound, while he told me curious fragments of the life which was ended below. He mentioned no names—they would have meant nothing to me if he had—but he wrested the secret meaning out of each life, pouncing on it, holding it up with a certain racy enjoyment in his own astuteness. . . . I must confess that I think he forgot the country and its homage and me that morning, and talked simply for his own pleasure in his own pathos and fun, just as a woman might take out her jewels when she was alone, to hold up the glittering strings and take delight in their shining. Once, I remember, he halted by a magnificent shaft and read the bead roll of the virtues of the man who lay beneath: "A devoted husband, a tender father, a noble citizen—dying triumphant in the Christian faith."

"Now this dead man," he said, in a high, rasping tone, "was a prize fighter, a drunkard, and a thief. He beat his wife. But she puts up this stone. He had money!"

Then he hurried me across the slopes to an obscure corner where a grave was hidden by high, wild grasses. He knelt and parted the long branches. Under them was a little headstone with the initials "M. H.," and underneath the verse:

She lived unknown and few could know
When Mary ceased to be, but she is gone, and Oh!
The difference to me!

—*Bits of Gossip*, 1904

FOLLOW PROPER PRACTICE WHEN DEATH IS CAUSED BY DISEASE. Bodies of persons dying of smallpox, scarlet fever, diphtheria, membranous croup, or measles should be wrapped in several thicknesses of cloth wrung out of full-strength corrosive sublimate, carbolic, or formaldehyde solution and should not thereafter be exposed. The funeral should be private and no persons except the undertaker and his assistant, the clergyman, and the immediate family of the deceased should attend. Carriages used by persons attending the funeral ceremony should be fumigated. No person should enter the sick room until it has been thoroughly disinfected.

PREVENT BURYING A LOVED ONE ALIVE. Since there are no reliable methods for determining death and since new chemical and industrial methods of putting people in comas are multiplying in society, the fear of burial alive is very real. There have been reports of corpses exhumed with hair and nails grown long and fingernail scratches in the coffin lid. The reader is directed to a recently patented improved burial case. The nature of this invention consists in placing on the lid of the coffin, and directly over the face of the body laid therein, a square tube, which extends from the coffin up through and over the surface of the grave, said tube containing a ladder and a cord, one end of said cord being placed in the hand of the person laid in the coffin, and the other end of said cord being attached to a bell on the top of the square tube; so that, should a person be interred ere life is extinct, he can, on recovery to consciousness, ascend from the grave and the coffin by the ladder; or, if not able to ascend by said ladder, ring the bell, thereby giving an alarm, and thus save himself from premature burial and death; and if, on inspection, life is extinct, the tube is withdrawn, the sliding door closed, and the tube used for a similar purpose.

 # BIBLIOGRAPHY

BOOKS AND ARTICLES

American Stove Co., Publishers. *Cook Book: "New Process" Wick Oil Cook Stove.* American Stove Co., Publishers, ca. 1910. At: Emergence of Advertising in America: 1850–1920 (see websites).

Barnes, Demas. *From the Atlantic to the Pacific, Overland Via the Overland Stage, 1865: A Series of Letters.* New York: D. Van Norstrand, 1866.

Beebe, Katherine. *Home Occupations for Little Children.* Chicago: The Werner Company, 1896.

Beecher, Catherine E., and Harriet Beecher Stowe. *The American Woman's Home, or Principles of Domestic Science.* New York: J.B. Ford, 1869.

Bird, Isabella L. *A Lady's Life in the Rocky Mountains.* New York: G.P. Putnam's Sons, 1881. At: Victorian Women Writers Project (see websites).

Block, August Hauck Collection. Box 4, Fed. 59, Archives University of Colorado at Boulder Libraries.

Buss, Amelia Butts (Mrs. George). *Diary, 1866-1867.* SMss Drawer, Archives University of Colorado at Boulder Libraries.

California Fruit Growers Exchange, Publishers. *Recipes for Dainty Dishes: Culinary Toilet, and Medicinal Hints.* California Fruit Growers Exchange, ca. 1910s. At: Emergence of Advertising in America: 1850–1920 (see websites).

"Calling Card Etiquette," *The Delineator.* At: Victoriana.Com Study Center (see websites).

Cary, Phoebe. "The Two Lovers," *Appletons' Journal: A Magazine of General Literature,* Vol. 5, Issue 102, March 11, 1871. At: Making of America (see websites).

Chase, A.W., M.D. *Dr. Chase's Third Last and Complete Receipt Book and Household Physician (Memorial Edition).* Detroit: F.B. Dickerson Company, 1903.

Church & Dwight Co., Publishers. *Cow Brand Soda Cook Book and Facts Worth Knowing, Established Half a Century.* New York: Church & Dwight Co., 1900. At: Emergence of Advertising in America: 1850–1920 (see websites).

C. I. Hood & Co. Apothecaries, Publishers. *Hood's Cook Book Reprint Number One.* L owell, MA: C. I. Hood & Co., post 1877. At: Emergence of Advertising in America: 1850–1920 (see websites).

Cooper, Sarah B. "Ideal Womanhood," *Overland Monthly and Out West Magazine,* Vol. 7, Issue 4, October 1871. At: Making of America (see websites).

Corson, Juliet. *Miss Corson's Practical American Cookery and Household Management.* New York: Dodd, Mead, and Company, 1885.

Craik, Dinah Maria Mulock. *A Woman's Thoughts About Women.* London: Hurst and Blackett, 1858. At: Victorian Women Writers Project (see websites).

Crane, Rev. Jonathan Townley. *Popular Amusements.* Cincinnati: Hitchcock and Walden, 1870. At: Making of America (see websites).

Curtis, Isabel Gordon. *Mrs. Curtis's Cook Book: A Manual of Instruction in the Art of Everyday Cookery.* Petersburg, N.Y.: The Success Company, 1909.

Custer County Women's Club. *Reflections: Bicentennial-Centennial.* Colorado Springs: Copies Ltd. 1976. Western History Collection: Denver Public Library.

Darley Family Papers, 186?. Box 3, Folders 14 and 15, University of Colorado at Boulder Libraries.

Davis, Rebecca Harding. *Bits of Gossip.* Boston and New York: Houghton, Mifflin & Company and Cambridge: The Riverside Press, 1904. At: University of North Carolina's Documenting the American South Collection (see websites).

Eaton, Seymour. "Slips of Tongue and Pen, Lesson No. 28," *Self-Help and Home-Study,* Vol. 1, No. 5, Boston: Seymour Eaton, January, 1898.

Drew, Grace E. "Art and Fashion in Dinner-Giving." *Godey's Lady's Book,* December 1896. At: Godey's Lady's Book On-Line (see websites).

Farmer, Fannie Merritt. *Catering for Special Occasions.* Philadelphia: David McKay, 1911.

Farmer, Fannie Merritt. *The Boston Cooking-School Cook Book.* Boston: Little, Brown, and Company, 1896. Reprint, Mineola, NY: Dover Publications, Inc., 1997.

"Fashions in Calling Cards," *Harper's Bazar,* 1868. At: Victoriana.Com Study Center (see websites).

First Congregational Church of Colorado Springs, Colorado. *Recipes,* ca. 1920. Special Collections, Tutt Library, Colorado College, Colorado Springs, Colorado.

Fossett, Frank. *Colorado: A Historical, Descriptive and Statistical Work on the Rocky Mountain Gold and Silver Mining Region.* Denver: Daily Tribune Steam Printing House, 1876.

Fowler, Prof. O.S. "Posture and Kindred Signs Express Existing Sexual States," *Private Lectures on Perfect Men, Women and Children,* 1880. At: Victoriana.Com Study Center (see websites).

Freemont, Jessie Benton. *Far-West Sketches.* Boston: D. Lothrop Company, 1890. At: American Memory (see websites).

French, Celia M. "Aunt Sally's Home." *Ladies' Repository: A Monthly Periodical, Devoted to Literature, Arts, and Religion,* Vol. 11, Issue 2. Cincinnati: Methodist Episcopal Church, 1873. At: Making of America (see websites).

Dick & Fitzgerald, Publishers. *Athletic Sports for Boys: A Repository of Graceful Recreations for Youth.* New York: Dick & Fitzgerald, 1866. At: Making of America (see websites).

D. Ransom Son & Co., Publishers. *Ransom's Family Receipt Book.* Buffalo, NY: D. Ransom Son & Co., 1885. At: Emergence of Advertising in America: 1850–1920 (see websites).

Elliott, Mrs. Sarah A. *Mrs. Elliott's Housewife, Containing Practical Receipts in Cookery.* New York: Hurd and Houghton, 1870.

French, Celia M. "Aunt Sally's Home," *Ladies' Repository: A Monthly Periodical, Devoted to Literature, Arts, and Religion,* Vol. 11, Issue 2. Cincinnati: Methodist Episcopal Church, 1873. At: Making of America (see websites).

Gillette, Mrs. F.L., and Hugo Ziemann. *The White House Cook Book.* Chicago: The Werner Company, 1887. Reprint, Ottenheimer Publishers, Inc., 1999.

Hammond, S. H. and L. W. Mansfield. *Country Margins and Rambles of a Journalist,* New York: J.C. Derby, 1855. At: The On-Line Books Page (see websites).

Harland, Marion. *Common Sense in the Household: A Manual of Practical Housewifery.* New York: Charles Scribner & Co., 1871.

Harper & Brothers, Publishers. "Cotton for Dresses," *Harper's New Monthly Magazine,* Vol. xxxvi (December 1867–May 1868), 611–12, New York: Harper & Brothers, Publishers, 1868.

Harper & Brothers, Publishers. "Editor's Drawer," *Harper's New Monthly Magazine,* Vol. xxxvi (December, 1867–May, 1868), 266, 673. New York: Harper & Brothers, Publishers, 1868.

Harper & Brothers, Publishers. "Etiquette," *Harper's New Monthly Magazine,* Vol. xxxvi (Dec. 1867–May 1868), 384–87. New York: Harper & Brothers, Publishers, 1868.

Hartshorne, Henry, M.D. *The Household Cyclopedia of General Information Containing over Ten Thousand Receipts in All the Useful and Domestic Arts.* Philadelphia: T. Ellwood Zell and Pittsfield, MA: J. Brainard Clarke, 1871.

Hayes, Rutherford B. *White House Diary Entry,* March 18, 1878. At: The Ohio Historical Society (see websites).

"Hints for Plains Travelers," *Omaha Herald,* 1877. At: Wells Fargo (see websites).

Housel, Will. *Senior Class Day Poem: University of Colorado.* University Portfolio, Vol. VII #3, May, 1889. At: Notable Women Ancestors (see websites).

Ingersoll, Ernest. *The Crest of the Continent: A Summer's Ramble in the Rocky Mountains and Beyond.* Chicago: R. R. Donnelley & Sons, 1885.

International Health Resort, Publishers. *International Health Resort Recipes.* Chicago: International Health Resort, ca. 1900. At: Emergence of Advertising in America: 1850–1920 (see websites).

J.D. Larkin & Co., Publishers. *Sweet Home Cook Book.* Buffalo, NY: 1888. Reprint, Paducah, KY: Image Graphics, Inc.

Jeffries, Prof. B.G., and J.L. Nichols. *The Household Guide or Domestic Cyclopedia.* Naperville, IL: J.L. Nichols & Co., 1902.

Johnson, Helen Louise. *The Enterprising Housekeeper, Suggestions for Breakfast, Luncheon, and Supper 2nd ed.* Philadelphia: The Enterprise Manufacturing Co., 1898. At: Emergence of Advertising in America: 1850–1920 (see websites).

Johnson, Sophia Orne [aka "Daisy Eyebright"]. *A Manual of Etiquette with Hints on Politeness and Good Breeding.* Philadelphia: David McKay, Publisher, 1873. At: A Celebration of Women Writers (see websites).

Keary, A., E., and M. *Enchanted Tulips and Other Verses for Children.* London: Macmillan and Co., 1914. At: A Celebration of Women's Writers (see websites).

Kingsley, Charles [Hrsg.], ed. *South by West or Winter in the Rocky Mountains and Spring in Mexico.* London: W. Isbister & Company, 1874. At: Gottinger Digitalisierungs-Zentrum (see websites).

Ladies Aid Society, First M.E. Church. *Good Housekeeping in High Altitudes.* Colorado Springs, Colo. 1888. Western History Collection: Denver Public Library.

Ladies' Aid Society of Denver Friends Church. *The Denver Quaker Cook Book: A collection of thoroughly tried recipes…modified as to be adapted to the altitude of Colorado.* North Denver, Colo.: Alexander & Meyer, Printers, 1905.

Ladies of Congregational Church. *Cloud City Cook-Book.* Leadville, Colorado. 1889. Western History Collection: Denver Public Library.

Ladies of St. Mark's Ladies Aid Society. *Our Kitchen Friend. Compiled From Tried Recipes Contributed by the Ladies of St. Mark's Ladies Aid Society.* Denver: The Society, ca. 1889. Special Collections Department University of Denver.

Ladies of the Church. *The Twenty-Third Avenue Presbyterian Cook Book.* Denver: The Merchants Publishing Co., 1897. Special Collections Department, University of Denver.

Ladies of the First Baptist Church. *How We Cook in Colorado. Choice Recipes Contributed by the Ladies of the First Baptist Church.* Denver, 1907. Special Collections Department, University of Denver.

Ladies of the Gypsum Methodist Episcopal Church. *Western Slope Cook Book.* Eagle, Colo.: George T. Haubrich (ed.), 1912. Western History Collection: Denver Public Library.

Ladies of the Presbyterian Golden Circle. *The Golden Circle Cook Book.* Longmont, Colorado, 1909. Western History Collection: Denver Public Library.

Leader. *The Mesa Workers' Cook Book.* Colorado: Mesa Workers of the Mesa Presbyterian Church of Pueblo, Colorado, 1897. Special Collections Department, University of Denver.

Lecompte, Janet (ed.). *Emily—The Diary of a Hard-Worked Woman by Emily French.* Lincoln and London: The University of Nebraska Press, 1987.

Logan, Olive (Mrs. Wirt Sikes). *Get thee behind me, Satan! A home-born book of home-truths.* New York: Adams, Victor & Co., 1872. At: Making of America (see websites).

Lydia E. Pinkham, Medicine Co. "Fruits and Candies," ca. 1900s. At: Emergence of Advertising in America: 1850–1920 (see websites).

MacCarthy, Brendan. "Home-Life in Colorado," *Catholic World,* Vol. 40, Issue 237, December 1884. At: Making of America (see websites).

Mallon, Isabel A. "The Small Belongings of Dress," *The Ladies' Home Journal,* April 1894. At: The Costume Gallery (see websites).

Mariager, Dagmar. "Camp and Travel in Colorado," *Overland Monthly and Out West Magazine,* Vol. 15, Issue 89, January 1890. At: Making of America (see websites).

Miss Beecher's Housekeeper and Healthkeeper: Containing Five Hundred Recipes for Economical and Healthful Cooking; also Many Directions for Securing Health and Happiness. New York: Harper Brothers, Publishers, 1873. At: Making of America (see websites)

"Mourning and Funeral Usages," *Harper's Bazar,* April 17, 1886. At: Victoriana.Com Study Center (see websites).

Myers, Mrs. E. G. *The Capitol Cook Book, a Selection of Tested Recipes, by the Ladies of Albert Sidney Johnston Chapter, Daughters of the Confederacy.* Austin, TX: Van Boeckmann. Schutze & Company, Printers, 1899. Reprint, *The Capitol Cookbook, a Facsimile of the Austin 1899 Edition.* Austin, TX: State House Press, 1995.

Norton, Caroline Trask. *The Rocky Mountain Cook Book for High Altitude Cooking.* Denver, Colo.: Caroline Trask Norton, 1903.

O'Rell, Max. "Studies in Cheerfulness—I," *The North American Review,* Vol. 167, Issue 505, December, 1898. Cedar Falls, IA: University of Northern Iowa.

Philalethean Club. *The Philalethean Cook Book.* Montrose Colorado: 1911. Special Collections Department, University of Denver.

Price Flavoring Extract Co. *Dr. Price's Delicious Desserts.* Chicago: Price Flavoring Extract Co., 1904. At: Emergence of Advertising in America: 1850–1920 (see websites).

Rorer, Sarah Tyson. *Cereal Foods and How to Cook Them.* Chicago: American Cereal Company, 1899. At: Emergence of Advertising in America: 1850–1920 (see websites).

Seely, Mrs. L. *Mrs. Seely's Cook Book: A Manual of French and American Cookery.* New York: The MacMillan Company, 1902.

Shafroth, Virginia M. *Round Table Cook Book.* Denver: State of Colorado—Executive Chamber, 1910. Western History Collection, Denver Public Library.

Siringo, Charles A. *A Texas Cowboy of Fifteen Years on the Hurricane Deck of a Spanish Pony—Taken from Real Life.* William Sloane Associates, 1886. Western Americana Collection of The Beinecke Rare Book and Manuscript Library, Yale University Library.

Sloan, Dr. Earl S. *Sloan's Cook Book and Advice to Housekeepers* (Recipes and Advertisements for Remedies Manufactured by Dr. Earl S. Sloan at 615 Albany Street and 111 East Brookline Street, Boston). Boston: F. E. Bacon & Co. Printers, 1905. At: Emergence of Advertising in America: 1850–1920 (see websites).

Stoddard, Elizabeth. "The Tea-Party," *Appletons' Journal: A Magazine of General Literature,* Vol. 6, Issue 132, October 7, 1871. New York: D. Appleton and Company. At: Making of America (see websites).

Stopes, Marie C. *Married Love.* London: G.P. Putnam Sons, 1918. At: A Celebration of Women's Writers (see websites).

Stowe, Harriet Beecher. *House and Home Papers.* Boston: Fields, Osgood, & Co, 1869. At: Making of America (see websites).

"Styles of the Month for Children," *McCall's Magazine,* Vol. xxxv, No. 9, May 1908.

At: The Costume Gallery (see websites).

"Teaching Table Manners," *The Ladies' Repository: A Monthly Periodical, Devoted to Literature, Arts, and Religion,* Vol. 25, Is. 2 (February, 1865). Cincinnati: Methodist Episcopal Church. At: Making of America (see websites).

Tyree, Marion Cabell. *Housekeeping in Old Virginia.* Louisville, KY: John P. Morton & Co., 1879.

W. M. Underwood Co., Publishers. *Taste the Taste and Some Cookery News.* Boston: W. M. Underwood Co., ca 1910. At: Emergence of Advertising in America: 1850–1920 (see websites).

Wade, Samuel. Quoted from the *Colorado Farmer,* November 12, 1885, in Steinel, Alvin T., *History of Agriculture in Colorado.* Fort Collins, 1926. 507-508.

Webb, William Edward. *Buffalo Land: An Authentic Account of the Discoveries, Adventures, and Mishaps of a Scientific and Sporting Party in the Wild West.* Cincinnati and Chicago: E. Hannaford & Company, 1872. At: Nineteenth Century in Print (see websites).

White, Mrs. Anna R. *Youth's Educator for Home and Society.* Chicago: Union Publishing House, 1896. At: Rochester History Department's Home Page: Youth's Educator for Home and Society (see websites).

Willard, Frances E. A *Wheel Within a Wheel: How I Learned to Ride the Bicycle (With Some Reflections by the Way).* Fleming H. Revell Co., 1895. Reprint, Bedford, MA: Applewood Books.

Women of the First Congregational Church of Marysville, Ohio. *Centennial Buckeye Cook Book.* Marysville, OH: J.H. Shearer & Son, 1876. Reprint, *Centennial Buckeye Cook Book Originally Published in 1876,* with an introduction and appendices by Andrew F. Smith, Columbus: Ohio State University Press, 2000.

Wood-Allen, M.D., Mary and Sylvanus Stall, D.D. *What a Young Woman Ought to Know.* Philadelphia & London: Vir Publishing Company, 1898.

The Woman's Book, vol. 2. New York: Charles Scribner's Sons, 1894.

Wright, A. S. *Wright's book of 3000 practical receipts.* New York: Dick & Fitzgerald, 1869. At: Making of America (see websites).

WEBSITES

19th Century Harpers Bazar Magazine
www.victoriana.com/library/harpers/harpers.html

19th Century Scientific American Online

www.history.rochester.edu/Scientific_American

American Memory: Historical Collections for the National Digital Library
http://memory.loc.gov/

A Celebration of Women Writers
http://digital.library.upenn.edu/women/writers.html

The Costume Gallery   www.costumegallery.com

Emergence of Advertising in America: 1850–1920   http://scriptorum.lib.duke.edu/eaa/

Godey's Lady's Book On-Line   http://www.history.rochester.edu/godeys/

Goettinger Digitalisierungs-Zentrum   http://www.sub.uni-goettingen.de/index-e.html

Her Heritage   www.plgrm.com/Heritage/women/

Household Words: Women Write for and from the Kitchen, featuring the collection of
the Walter H. & Leonore Annenberg Rare Book & Manuscript Library of the University of Pennsylvania.   www.library.upenn.edu/special/gallery/aresty/aresty22.html

Making of America Project   http://moa.umdl.umich.edu or
moa.cit.cornell.edu/moa/index.html

Nineteenth Century in Print   http://memory.loc.gov

Notable Women Ancestors   http://www.rootsweb.com/

The Ohio Historical Society   www.ohiohistory.org

The On-Line Books Page   http://digital.library.upenn.edu/books

Overland Trail   http://www.over-land.com/diarybarnes.html

Pilgrim New Media   www.plgrm.com

Rochester History Department's Youth's Educator for Home and Society Page
www.history.rochester.edu/ehp-book/yefhas

State University of New York at Binghamton
http://womhist.binghamton.edu

University of North Carolina at Chapel Hill Libraries Documenting the American
South Collection   docsouth.unc.edu/southlit/southlit.html

Victorian Women Writers Project   http://www.indiana.edu/~letrs/vwwp/

Victoriana.Com Study Center   www.victoriana.com

Wells Fargo   www.wellsfargo.com

INDEX